Northern Ontario:
There's More To Northern Ontario Than Just Rocks, Trees and Lakes

A humourous look at the history and some of the places of Northern Ontario. Not all of the places. There are 387 places in Northern Ontario, not counting all the places where there are no people and which are therefore difficult to count as official places. Anyway, 387 places is a lot of places. And you can only put so many places into one little book.

by Geoffrey Corfield

drawings by

DESPUB

© 2002 DESPUB/David E. Scott
© 2002 Geoffrey Corfield
© Typefaces by Corel

Printed and bound in Canada
All rights reserved. No part of this work covered by the copyright hereon may be reproduced or used in any form or by any means – electronic, graphical or mechanical – without the written permission of the publisher, except for reviewers, who may quote brief passages. Any request for photocopying, recording, taping or storage on an information retrieval system of any part of this work shall be directed in writing to the publisher.

The Publisher: DESPUB
2340B Clifton Street
Allanburg, Ontario, Canada L0S 1A0

National Library of Canada Cataloguing in Publication Data
Corfield, Geoffrey, 1949-
Main entry under title:
Northern Ontario: There's More To Northern Ontario Than Just Rocks, Trees and Lakes

Includes index.
ISBN 0-9688996-5-X

1. Northern Ontario (Ont.) -- History--Humour. 1. Title

FC3094.4.C672002   971.3'1'00207   C2002-901195-7
F1058.C67 2002

Editing/design:	David E. Scott
Printing:	AGMV Marquis
Cover & Illustrations:	Inkblot/Geoffrey Corfield
Layout	Pat Dracup

A DESPUB publication

Table of Contents

1) North 5
2) Northern Ontario 7
3) North Bay 10
4) How To Stake a Mining Claim 16
5) Temiskaming, Timiskaming or Temiscaming . . . 19
6) Hockey 29
7) Timmins 31
8) The Polar Bear Express 39
9) Sudbury 43
10) Elliot Lake: The Colossal Rise, Rather Big Fall, and Gradual Rise Again of Elliot Lake . . . 53
11) Sault Ste. Marie 63
12) The Group of Seven 73
13) The Algoma Central Railway 77
14) Wawa 79
15) Black Bear White River 81
16) Black Flies 83
17) Parks 85
18) Lake Superior 88
19) Thunder Bay: A Fort and a Port and a Last Resort 91
20) The Land on the Other Side of the Time Zone . . 101
21) Red Lake 105
22) Kenora 113

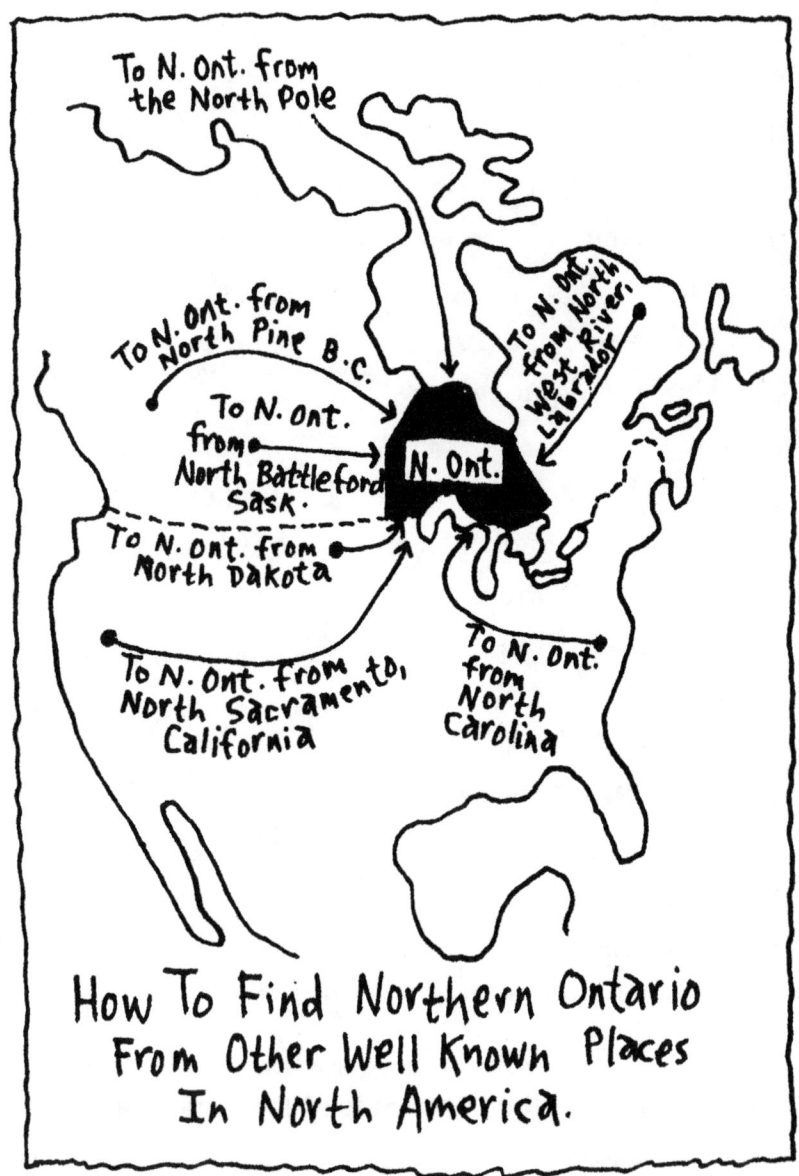

CHAPTER ONE

North

Canada is a land of "north." It stretches from Pelee Island north to the North Pole. But in between there are many different levels of north, each one more north than the last one.

To the people of Southwestern Ontario, north is Georgian Bay. To the people of Toronto, north is North Bay. To the people of North Bay, north is James Bay. To the people of James Bay, north is Hudson Bay. To the people of Hudson Bay, north is Arctic Bay. To the people of Arctic Bay north is the North Pole. And there north ends. There is no more north. It's all south after that. Downhill south all the way. But on the way up north there have been quite a few levels of north along the way. Stepping-stones north.

North occurs in every province and territory in Canada. Even Prince Edward Island, which is more east-west than north-south, has some north in it. It has a north shore and a south shore.

To the people of Southern Ontario, Northern Ontario is north. To the people of Northern Canada, Northern Ontario is south. But to the people of the rest of Canada, Northern Ontario is just plain ordinary Canada.

Every other province in Canada has some north in it which is more north than North Bay, Ontario. All the major cities of western Canada (except Victoria), are north of Hearst, Ontario, which in Northern Ontario is just about as far north as you can go. Yet seen from Point Pelee, Hearst is really north.

Canada is a country of north. You can't get away from it. North is always there. On top of you. In layers. Of all the provinces only Quebec has more north-south in it than Ontario has. But it's the oddball shape and geography of Ontario that makes its north-south so different. Ontario has the most dramatic north-south divide in it of any part of Canada. Ontario separates itself into north and south easier than any other province. There is a Southern Ontario and there is a Northern Ontario. And they are two quite different Ontarios.

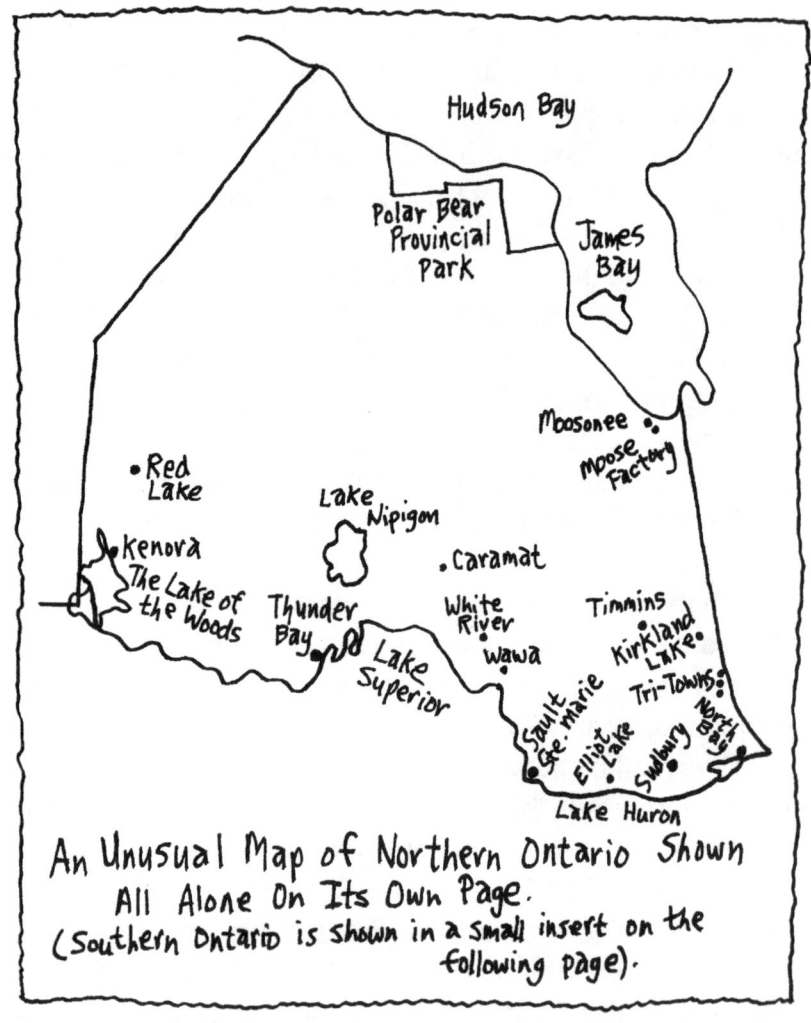

An Unusual Map of Northern Ontario Shown All Alone On Its Own Page. (Southern Ontario is shown in a small insert on the following page).

Chapter Two

Northern Ontario

Ontario is a funny province. It curls around the lower Great Lakes and hugs the south bank of the Ottawa River, then squishes itself into a narrow gooseneck of land 160 kilometres (100 miles) wide with Lake Nipissing in the middle of it, before absolutely exploding out north and west into its huge northern area.

Map Showing Northern Ontario and its Tiny Southern Ontario Attachment.

To the south of this gooseneck is the most heavily populated region in Canada. To the north is one of the most lightly populated.

To the south the rocks, trees and lakes gradually give way and the land becomes flat and full of farms, towns and cities. To the north the rocks, trees and lakes are just starting to get going and the land is rugged and not full of farms, towns and cities at all.

To the south there are roads that become more numerous and get closer and closer together. To the north there are a few roads and they get fewer and fewer and further and further apart. And then disappear altogether.

To the south there are big cities which appear to be smaller than they are because there are more of them. To the north there are small cities which appear to be bigger than they are because there aren't that many of them.

To the south is Southern Ontario. To the north is

Northern Ontario. Southern Ontario has 11% of the land area of Ontario and 96% of the people. Northern Ontario has 89% of the land and 4% of the people. Two quite different Ontarios.

The Trans-Canada Highway runs north from North Bay 376 Kilometres (235 miles) to Cochrane and then turns west. It doesn't go any further north. But just look at how much more north there is! Northern Ontario goes north another 720 kilometres (450 miles) from Cochrane to Hudson Bay. Hudson Bay! Hudson Bay empties into the Arctic Ocean! Polar bears live on Hudson Bay! Henry Hudson got lost on Hudson Bay! Hudson Bay is completely different from Toronto! It's a whole different world up here!

Northern Ontario is different. Yet it's still Ontario. Northern Ontario is 1,280 kilometres (800 miles) across from Ingolf in the west to Mattawa in the east, and 1,360 kilometres (850 miles) up and down from Killarney in the south to north of Fort Severn. Northern Ontario is big. It's bigger than France and Germany put together. Bigger than Texas. Bigger than Manitoba, Saskatchewan, Alberta or British Columbia. And 168 times bigger than Prince Edward Island.

Northern Ontario is big. In fact if there were any part of Canada where you might be tempted to create a new province, then Northern Ontario is it. If there can be a new territory (Nunavut), there could be a new province. If Prince Edward Island can have a provincial capital, Northern Ontario could too.

But if there were to be a Province of Northern Ontario, where would its capital be? The mid-point of Northern Ontario is Caramat, 45 kilometres (28 miles) southeast of Longlac. So if you wanted your new provincial capital to be in the middle of your new province, then Caramat would be it. (The name Caramat is formed by reversing the letters of the French word tamarac, an indigenous tree).

But Thunder Bay, Sudbury and Sault Ste. Marie would want to be the provincial capital too. So how should we decide? It would be quite a scrap. Leave it up to the Queen? There'd be quite a scrap over that as well.

So all in all things are probably just best left as they are. For now anyway. Northern Ontario: The Closest Thing To Being A Province In Canada We Have Without Actually Being A Province. Northern Ontario: Canada's Most Worthy Unannointed Province. Northern Ontario: Canada's Province-In-Waiting.

In Northern Ontario they don't play the game "Rock-Paper-Scissors," they play the game "Rocks-Trees-Lakes" (it's a regional adaptation). The Rock (clenched fist) crushes the Tree (open fingers). The Tree floats on the Lake (flat palm). And the Lake swallows the Rock. It's a different world all right is Northern Ontario.

Chapter Three

North Bay

North Bay is in that gooseneck of land between Northern Ontario and Southern Ontario. North Bay is at the north end of Southern Ontario and the south end of Northern Ontario. North Bay has a foot in both Ontarios.

North Bay calls itself "The Gateway of the North." But it could be called "The Gateway of the South" too. It just depends upon which way you're going. And which gateway you're going through.

If you're going through the gateway between Lake Nipissing and Quebec, then you'll see North Bay because it's in that gateway. But if you're going through the gateway between Lake Nipissing and Georgian Bay, then you'll miss North Bay because it's not in that gateway (you'll just have to make do with Bigwood or French River instead).

Lake Nipissing sits right in the middle of these two gateways between Northern and Southern Ontario. Lake Nipissing is a lake that hardly anybody thinks about. But Lake Nipissing is no puddle. It's 896 square kilometres (350 square miles) of lake. A lake almost six times as big as Liechtenstein. A lake bigger than the islands of Grenada, Bermuda and Barbados combined (but without the coral reefs).

North Bay is on Lake Nipissing. On the northeast shore of Lake Nipissing. But not on North Bay bay. Because there is no North Bay bay on Lake Nipissing. There's a Great North Bay bay, but the city of North Bay's not on it. There's a West Bay, and a South Bay, and a bay that should be called East Bay but isn't (it's called Callander Bay instead); but there's no North Bay bay. The city of North Bay's not on a bay at all. It's on a fairly straight stretch of Lake Nipissing shoreline.

Anyway they called the place North Bay because an early settler ordered nails from Pembroke and asked that they be shipped to "the north bay of Lake Nipissing." He's lucky they arrived at all. With a delivery address like that they should have ended up on Great North Bay bay. But they didn't. They ended up in North Bay and North Bay ended up with the name North Bay.

A North Bay Hearse Sleigh 1907, black only, shown empty (sleigh built with nails from Pembroke).

North Bay the name may have started with an order for nails, but North Bay the town was started by French fur traders. Étienne Brûlé was the first to discover what would become part of the famous voyageur fur trade route: up the Ottawa River to Mattawa, turn left, up the Mattawa River to Trout Lake, and then portage and paddle 7 kilometres (4.5 miles) to Lake Nipissing.

They had to portage between Trout Lake and Lake Nipissing because Trout Lake was higher and flowed east, while Lake Nipissing flowed west. The portage was a muddy one. So they called the river that flowed into Lake Nipissing "La Rivière Vase" (Mud River), and their trading post on this river "La Vase" (Mud). So North Bay's first name was Mud.

It's second name was "Fort La Ronde" which was quite an improvement. But when the voyageurs stopped paddling Fort La Ronde was closed in 1821. (The fur trade eventually came back to North Bay however, and today North Bay holds one of the world's largest international auctions of wild furs).

Nothing further happened at North Bay until the railway came along in 1882 and built a depot at Nipissing Junction (south part of the city). And then the settlers came. But most of them settled a little further north along the lake (Oak Street), and closer to Trout Lake (to be out of the mud). And then came the order for nails. And then came the name. And then came North Bay.

When the District of Nipissing was formed in 1889, North Bay was voted its administrative centre. That same year North Bay became a town, only the third incorporated town in Northern Ontario after Port Arthur and Sault Ste. Marie. North Bay had come a long way in a short time. Other than being a railway stop, lake port and government office, North Bay was also a lumbering town with saw mills, lumber camps, steam boats, and lumbermen wearing "Riverman's Caulk Boots" (no sizes, just try them on until you find a pair that fit).

But North Bay was not going to be your average Northern Ontario town. North Bay was going to be something different. North Bay was going to be something more ordinary. A regular town. Not a one job resource town. A normal town with a normal variety of jobs. A town with no booms and busts. A town that didn't live or die by the stock market. A town with no mass comings and goings. A town without the exciting existence of a lot of other Northern Ontario towns perhaps, but a town with a bit more stability in the long run. Other towns would have the "mining camps" and the "rushes" and all the excitement. And they did.

They found silver at Cobalt and gold at Larder Lake, Swastika and Timmins. And the railway went north to them.

And their supplies went north to them on the railway from North Bay. Harry Oakes, Benny Hollinger, Noah Timmins and Sandy McIntyre went north to find fortunes or to find fortunes for others. And the railway took them there. And they probably got out and stretched their legs at North Bay. Maybe even bought a pair of Caulk Boots.

North Bay was not your rip-roaring "Sudbury Saturday Night" kind of town. With a population of 7,000 in 1909, North Bay had only two policemen. North Bay was the law-abiding link between Southern Ontario and the "New Ontario" to the north.

But the idea of the old east-west link had not completely died away. In 1837 the government studied the idea of a "ship canal between Georgian Bay and the Ottawa River." In 1907 they issued a report on it. It would require 25 less locks and 365 less kilometres (228 miles) than the St. Lawrence Seaway. The idea also came up in 1903, 1912 and 1920.

But the results were always the same. The St. Lawrence won out over Lake Nipissing. North Bay would not become a canal town. There would be no skating on the North Bay canal. No North Bay rowing regatta. But even without a canal North Bay was described in 1910 as "one of the most prosperous towns in New Ontario." Prosperity by being ordinary. Progress by being normal (North Bay even had a "Normal School").

The railway reached North Bay in 1882, but good quality roads were some way behind. In 1912 a North Bay family drove to Pembroke (probably not to buy nails), and had 31 flat tires (probably not all from nails). The 59 kilometres (37 miles) to Mattawa took half a day. By 1927 the highway reached as far north as Matheson, but you needed a permit to drive between North Bay and Temagami. It was that much of an adventure (it was like going down the Amazon or scaling Mount Everest).

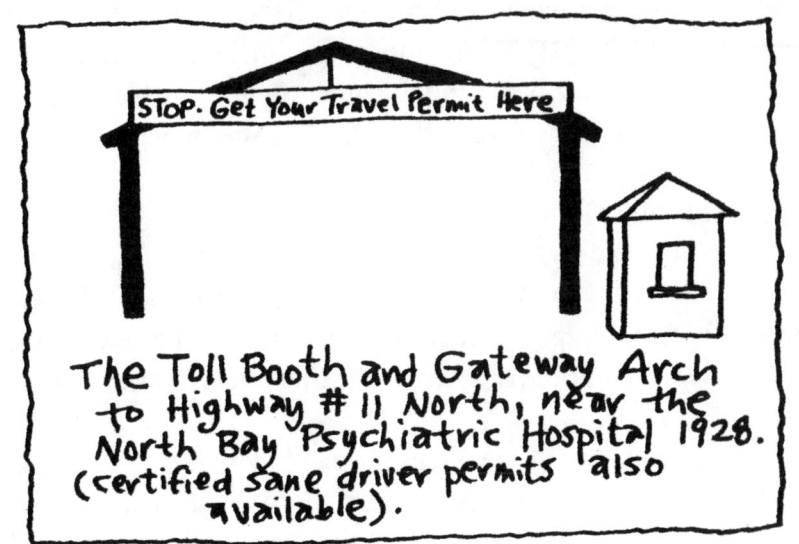

The Toll Booth and Gateway Arch to Highway #11 North, near the North Bay Psychiatric Hospital 1928. (certified sane driver permits also available).

In other Northern Ontario towns people became millionaires from mining. In North Bay they became millionaires by selling radios. In 1928 Roy Thomson was selling radios door-to-door in North Bay. Then he opened a radio station. Then he opened more. Then he opened a newspaper in Timmins. Then he opened more. Then he became a media tycoon. Then he became Lord Thomson of Fleet.

But in 1934 quiet, ordinary, radio-loving, normal North Bay suddenly got itself a real live worldwide tourist attraction. A family of five living on a small farm near Corbeil, Ontario (south of North Bay), had five more children. All at once.

The Dionne Quintuplets were not the first known set of quints to be born in the world. They were the first known set of quints to be born in the world to survive more than a few days. In 1934 the world was in a Depression. Any happy news was welcome. And what could be happier news than five baby girls born all at once for the first time!

The world adopted the Dionne Quintuplets. They became Canada's biggest tourist attraction overnight. The road north to Corbeil was paved for the Quints. Fearing for their celebrity status, the Ontario government took the Quints from their parents, set up a trust fund, and put them in a specially-built hospital and school where three million people paid to look at them behind one-way glass.

North Bay became "Quintland": souvenir stands, amusement parks, Hollywood. Not what you would expect from quiet, ordinary, radio-loving, normal North Bay. It was more excitement than any town in Canada had at that time. And it happened to a town that had until then only catered to the excitement of other towns.

But after things with the Quints quietened down a bit, North Bay went back to being Northern Ontario's successful ordinary town again. The Dionne Quintuplets' Home and Museum is today in downtown North Bay. Next to the Chamber of Commerce.

Quiet, ordinary, radio-loving, multiple-birthing, normal North Bay. A little bit of Southern Ontario in Northern Ontario. The last bit.

Chapter 4
How To Stake a Mining Claim

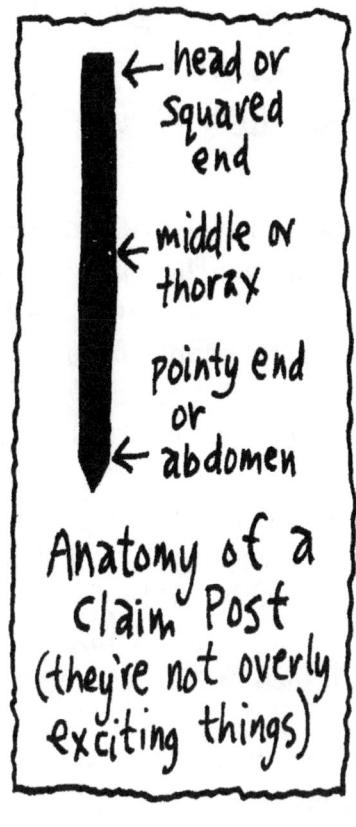

If there's one thing you need to know to understand the land north of North Bay, it's how to stake a mining claim. Staking a mining claim is what a lot of people originally came to Northern Ontario to do. Staking a mining claim determined where towns sprang up. Staking a mining claim determined who became millionaires and who didn't.

Northern Ontario is a land of mines and mining. But you didn't have to be a miner to make a fortune in mining. You could be a prospector too. Prospectors made fortunes by staking mining claims. Staking a mining claim is the first step in mining. If you staked a valuable claim where somebody wanted to mine, you could make a fortune by either selling your claim or taking a share in the mine. But best of all, you didn't need a fortune to be a prospector. Anyone could do it. All you needed was a hammer and a backpack and a stiff constitution. And the knowledge of how to stake a mining claim.

When mining claims were first being staked in Northern Ontario the maximum permitted size of a claim was 40 acres.

The province was divided into mining districts with a Mining Recorder's Office in each district, and each person was allowed to stake nine claims in each district.

In order to stake a mining claim you first needed a Miner's Licence available from any district office. Next you needed stakes of over four feet in length and squared at one end, the claim posts (or you could use trees cut to be posts). To stake your claim you put a claim post at each corner of the area you were staking, by either hammering it into the ground, or if the ground was frozen, solid rock or water, by somehow supporting the stake upright.

Early Prospecting Tools of the Trade.

On the squared end of each claim post you wrote: your name, mining licence number, date, time and number of post. The northeast post was always numbered #1. Southeast #2, Southwest #3, Northwest #4. You then cut a line (path) from one post to another. You have now staked your mining claim.

When this was done you then had to record your claim at the Mining Recorder's Office for the district in which your claim was staked, within 30 days of staking. The staker then had the right to work or sell the claim. There were of course fees for the licence and claim registration (there has to be something in this for the government).

To maintain the claim the claim holder had to perform a minimum of 40 days "assessment work" a year on the claim, for a total of 200 days work over five years, and register this work with the recording office (for some districts such as Kirkland Lake and Red Lake, this first 40 days work had to be done within the first 3 months, not the first year). If the claim holder did not record the required work within the time period, then the recording office would deem the claim expired or lapsed.

Staking a mining claim may sound like an orderly, tidy process. It wasn't. The Recording Offices were often not close to the areas being staked. Surveying lagged behind staking. Quite often the offices were swamped. How could they verify everything? The prospectors didn't always make nice, neat 40 acre squares. In fact hardly ever. They were all shapes and sizes. The stakes in the ground didn't always fit the lines on the map either. Claims overlapped. Little bits of land were left unclaimed in between claims. Somehow though the system muddled through.

In the end however it all came down to whether or not your claim was worth anything. And all the time you were staking claims you had to support yourself in an isolated area with a harsh climate. Being lucky helped of course. But to really make a fortune at prospecting you had to be more than just lucky. You had to be smart as well.

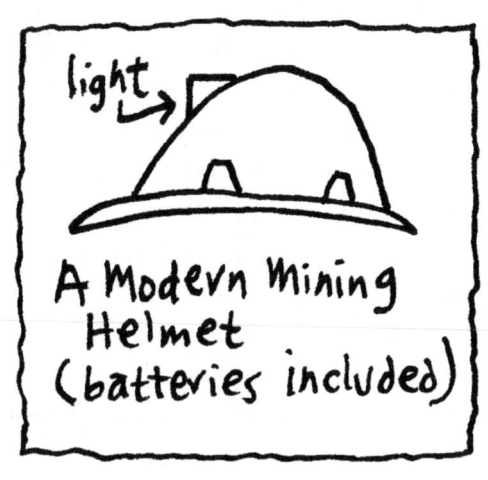

CHAPTER FIVE

Temiskaming, Timiskaming or Temiscaming

In a little corner of Northern Ontario sits the District of Timiskaming, one of Canada's best known mining areas and one with at least two or three official spellings (and probably more).

In the year 1900 though Timiskaming or Temiskaming or Temiscaming was hardly known at all. It was isolated and empty. No roads. No railway. Hardly any people. But the Ontario government wanted to attract people to come and live in these empty spaces north of North Bay, so they called this region "New Ontario" and began building a railway into it in 1903. (They didn't call it "North Ontario" because "north" meant cold and distant, and North Bay was already cold and distant enough. "New" was much better for attracting immigration).

They had found lead in Timiskaming in 1686 and iron ore in 1902, but nobody had paid any attention. It was however an omen. A sign of things to come. The area was loaded with minerals. It was just a matter of time. And then it happened.

Two railway workers found silver at Cobalt in 1903. Silver mixed with cobalt (a hard silvery-white metal used in alloys and to produce a blue colour in glass and ceramics). It lay on the ground "like stove-lids and cannonballs."

Progress on building the railway slowed as other workers rushed off to look for silver. The Cobalt Silver Rush however started slowly. But when some silver chunks were sent to Toronto in 1904, and Toronto saw the silver, the Cobalt Silver Rush was well and truly on.

Within one year there were 16 mines and thousands of prospectors. Within two years 100 mines. Within six years Cobalt had made more money than the Klondike and there were 3,000 people and 35 millionaires.

Cobalt was a wild place: tents, shacks, mud, tree stumps, mines. They drained Cobalt Lake and mined it. They mined the railway right-of-ways. Cobalt mining stocks traded in Toronto and New York. By 1908 Cobalt was the world's largest silver producer. But by 1920 most of the silver was gone, and most of the people were gone too. Cobalt though was the first of the Northern Ontario mining strikes. The first of many.

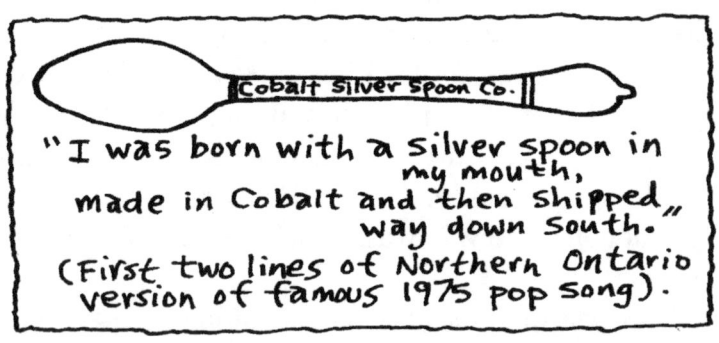

"I was born with a silver spoon in my mouth, made in Cobalt and then shipped way down south."
(First two lines of Northern Ontario version of famous 1975 pop song).

A town at Cobalt didn't actually start until disease epidemics caused by the mayhem forced it to. For before they found silver at Cobalt there were already two existing towns in Timiskaming just a little further north.

There had been a Hudson's Bay post at Haileybury since 1883. When the silver rush was on there was an Ontario liquor law which prohibited liquor being sold within eight kilometres (five miles) of a mine (Canada is famous for silly liquor laws). Cobalt was full of mines. So Cobalt couldn't have any bars. But there were no mines in Haileybury. And Haileybury was eight kilometres (five miles) from Cobalt. So people moved to

The Woods-Maguire Wedding Party Shown in Silhouette On a Front Porch in Haileybury 1900. (the porch is not far from a bar).

Haileybury to be beside Lake Timiskaming and near a bar.

Lakeshore Road in Haileybury became "Millionaires' Row." One person who didn't make a million in Haileybury however was author Leslie McFarlane, who wrote the first 21 books of the best-selling "Hardy Boys" series under the pen name Franklin W. Dixon for $100 a book. McFarlane was brought up in Haileybury and wrote 11 of the books here (he's in the Haileybury Heritage Museum).

The Tower Treasure
Franklin W. Dixon
The First Hardy Boys Book 1927.

When they built the railway north of Lake Timiskaming they found something else in the ground. Farm land. So there was a Farm Rush. They needed a farming town and New Liskeard was it. New Liskeard was one log cabin in 1891 and six log cabins in 1896. When the Silver Rush and the Farm Rush came along they just added more log cabins.

And so these three towns of Timiskaming grew up together: Cobalt, Haileybury, New Liskeard. In fact they grew up so much together that they became known as the "Tri-

Towns." The mining town, the farming town, and the town with all the money and the bars in the middle.

By 1906 the railway had been built as far north as Swastika when it happened again. They found gold at Larder Lake. GOLD! You couldn't get a better advertisement for immigration if you tried. Silver was one thing but gold was quite another. Gold made people pick up and immigrate at a moments notice. Gold fever hit Northern Ontario. Prospectors flooded in. The railway found customers. The province found immigrants. And some people even found gold.

(a) correct (b) incorrect
Drawing a Swastika the Swastika way.
(courtesy: School of Fine Swastikas, Swastica, Ont. P0K 1T0)

There were 4,000 claims staked at Larder Lake and "Larder City" was planned. But the gold was only surface gold and it soon ran out, and Larder City never happened.

Swastika was just a railway siding with no name when they found gold at Larder Lake. Then Bill and Jim Dusty found gold here and called their mine the "Swastika Mine." The story goes that they got this name from seeing a swastika charm on a necklace worn by a lady visiting the area. A fortunate sighting. There were not many lady visitors to Swastika wearing jewellery in 1906. But the name was good luck and the Swastika Mine was Northern Ontario's first important gold mine. They called the town Swastika after the mine.

When Adolf Hitler also adopted the swastika, the Ontario government sent somebody to Swastika in 1940 to try to persuade the village to change its name to something more patriotic, like "Winston." But Swastika kept its name: "Hitler be damned. This is our sign since 1922." You don't mess around with miners.

When the gold ran out at Larder Lake the prospectors headed for Swastika staking claims along the way. The surveyors followed. They had to survey to keep track of the claims. There were a lot of lakes they had to survey and name here, and there was one lake near Swastika that another lady played a part in naming.

Miss Winnifred Kirkland was a stenographer with the Ontario Land Surveys Branch of the Department of Lands and Forests in Toronto. They needed a name for this lake near Swastika. So they called it Kirkland Lake. It would be a name that would come to mean only one thing: GOLD! (not Miss Winnifred Kirkland).

But there was no Kirkland Lake gold Rush. Shortly after the Swastika strike came the Porcupine strike, and so most of the prospectors rushed off north and the Kirkland Lake claims expired and were forgotten. But not for long.

Bill Wright was born in England, joined the cavalry, and then bought a "Veteran's Lot" near Porcupine, Ontario, Canada from a Canadian veteran. In 1906 he came to Canada to see his "lot," found it was out in the middle of nowhere, and promptly went out west. Returning east in 1909 he persuaded his sister and her husband Ed Hargreaves to come to Canada and they settled in Colbalt where Bill and Ed did painting and decorating. But former cavalry soldiers do not make very good painters and decorators. They get bored quickly. Bill Wright got bored quickly, so when they found gold at Swastika he and Ed Hargreaves went off prospecting near Kirkland Lake even though they didn't know a single thing about it.

One day in 1911 they were shooting rabbits when they found gold. They staked four claims even though they didn't have the money to register them. Ed Hargreaves later sold his share in the claims for $7,500. Bill Wright later sold his "lot" near Porcupine to a mining company. The Wright-Hargreaves

Mine though became one of the richest gold mines in Kirkland Lake, and Bill Wright became a very wealthy former calvary private.

Harry Oakes was a professional prospector from Maine, U.S.A. who'd been prospecting in the Klondike Gold Rush, the Alaska Gold Rush, the California Gold Rush, the Mexican Gold rush, the New Zealand Gold Rush and the Australian Gold Rush. Harry Oakes had done a lot of gold rushing. He hadn't been lucky yet, but he was learning to be smart.

Oakes came to Timiskaming in 1911 and went straight to the Mining Recorder's Office in Matheson. Harry Oakes knew all about mining claims. He noticed that there were five claims near where Bill Wright had found gold that were due to expire at midnight on 7 January 1912. He struck a deal with the Tough brothers. If they would pay the claim fee he would split any takings from the claims with them. They agreed.

So on the night of 7 January they hiked 6.4 kilometres (four miles) out into the bush in -45°C weather and four feet of snow and re-staked these claims. It was a long, cold, hard night's work, but it would be worth it. Others had their eye on these claims too, but Harry Oakes had beaten them to it. They dug through the snow, rolled back the frozen moss, and found gold. The Tough-Oakes Mine would become one of Kirkland Lake's best gold mines too.

But Harry Oakes was still looking. He had a system. He plotted the surface veins of gold on a map. He roasted ore samples to see if they sweated gold. Then he staked claims where he thought the veins might be heading underground. And his map was leading him right to a lake.

He bought two claims near the lake cheaply and then waited a year for two more claims to expire so he could re-stake them. Only then did he register all four claims in his own name. Another of Harry Oakes's secrets was that he always kept everything a secret. He called this mine the Lakeshore Mine. The lake was Kirkland Lake. Not only would it become one of the richest gold mines in Kirkland Lake, it would become one of the richest gold mines in the world. It would make Harry Oakes rich. But not right away. There was still a lot of hard work to do. Finding gold on the surface was one thing, but digging it out of the ground was another.

Sandy McIntyre from Scotland came to Canada and discovered the McIntyre Mine, one of the richest gold mines in Timmins. Sandy McIntyre left his name on the McIntyre Mine, but Sandy McIntyre did not have anything else left from the McIntyre Mine. Four years after striking it rich he had blown it all away. Part of it blew the way of Jim Hughes who bought a ⅛ share of McIntyre's claim for $25.

Hughes also had some claims at Kirkland Lake. So he hired Sandy McIntyre to prospect it for him. Maybe McIntyre could find gold again? He did! Hughes gave McIntyre 150,000 shares in the Teck-Hughes Mine, but lightning also struck Sandy McIntyre twice the other way too. He sold his shares for

$4,500. They were eventually worth $1½ million. Sandy McIntyre had blown not one but two fortunes in gold.

Harry Oakes is squeezed for cash. So he sells all his shares in Tough-Oakes and ploughs everything he owns into Lakeshore. He is digging 270 feet down under the lake. Alone. Drill, blast, and haul it out with a bucket by climbing up and down ladders. Harry Oakes is going for the jackpot. And he hits it! Harry Oakes never has to worry about being squeezed for cash again.

The Teck-Hughes Mine shares fall to 5¢, but "Handsome" Charley Dennison buys them up, keeps the mine going, and is another to make a fortune at Kirkland Lake.

Bill Wright still has a ¼ interest in the Wright-Hargreaves Mine when he goes off to World War I. When the war is over he is the richest private in Canada.

The Kirkland Lake mines were known for being deep (8,200 feet down, 2,400 kilometres (1,500 miles) of horizontal tunnels, 19 kilometres (12 miles) of vertical shafts). Out of them came 72 million tons of ore yielding 900 tons of gold. The gold was found a home for, but what do you do with the waste rock? They made roads with it. Later on when the process of extracting gold was better, they realized that the rock they had used for roads contained gold. But it was too late. Kirkland Lake was "The Town with Roads Paved On Gold."

When they ran out of roads to build they dumped the waste rock into the lake. By 1930 the lake had completely disappeared. There is no more Kirkland Lake lake. There is a baseball field where the lake used to be. But because it was silly to have a town named Kirkland Lake with no lake named Kirkland Lake, they named another lake Kirkland Lake. So now there is a Kirkland Lake near the town of Kirkland Lake once again.

At the time of the discoveries of Wright, Oakes and Hughes, Kirkland Lake was nothing more than clearings in the bush, trails, and a wagon road to Swastika. A town didn't actually get started until 1915 when the Ontario Land Surveys Branch (where Miss Kirkland worked), surveyed lots for a town and sold them at auction.

Charlie Chow bought a lot and opened a Chinese restaurant (all small towns in Canada have a Chinese restaurant, it's almost an official requirement). Chow took mining shares for meals. Most of them turned out to be only good for wallpaper, but some yielded quite a good return on an investment of bacon and eggs.

> **MENU**
> **Charlie Chow's**
> coffee ..... 5 shares
> toast ...... 5 shares
> bacon & eggs ... .25 shares
> pork chop ..... 25 shares
> egg roll ...... 10 shares
> dinner for one ... 30 shares

Rosie Brown bought a lot, opened a boarding house, and set the early trend in mining town ladies' fashion: long gingham dress and apron worn with an old dusty fur coat, man's peaked cap, and rubber boots. This ensemble worn all day every day winter or summer.

Bill Wright took his millions, paid for an extension to the Kirkland Lake hospital, bought a stable of race horses near Barrie, and became the first president of the Globe & Mail newspaper.

Harry Oakes took his millions, donated land for a church and the first school in Kirkland Lake, built an arena, and bought a set of encyclopedia and 80 pairs of skates for the school. He also built a chateau in Kirkland Lake and Oak Hall in Niagara Falls, and went off to Britain and became Sir Harry Oakes. In 1943 he was found murdered in his house in The Bahamas under mysterious circumstances still unsolved.

* * * * *

Although Timiskaming has all the outdoor attractions that most of Northern Ontario has, it's still best known for mining.

In Haileybury they have the Haileybury School of Mines. Unknown in most academic circles it may be, but in mining circles the Haileybury School of Mines is known around the world.

In Cobalt they have the Northern Ontario Mining Museum and the Cobalt Heritage Silver Trail, a self-guided tour of Cobalt's mines.

In Virginiatown on Larder Lake they have one of Canada's richest gold mines and an Underground Gold Mine Tour.

In Kirkland Lake you can visit the former Tough-Oakes Mine and the Kirkland Lake Museum of Northern History located in Harry Oakes's chateau.

Nobody knows however what became of Miss Winnifred Kirkland of the Ontario Land Surveys Branch of the Department of Lands and Forests in Toronto. However she had a lake that was named after quite a famous gold-mining town that was named after a former lake named after her.

CHAPTER SIX

Hockey

There is actually something else that Kirkland Lake is known for other than mining. Hockey players. There is a plaque in Kirkland Lake with the names on it of all the hockey players born in town who have played in the National Hockey League, the top professional hockey league in the world. There's over 50 names on that plaque. Kirkland Lake makes hockey players. And figure skaters. Toller Cranston, one of the best figure skaters in the world (and probably the most innovative), was also born in Kirkland Lake. When Harry Oakes built an arena and bought skates for all the school kids in Kirkland Lake, he really started something.

Haileybury Hockey Stockings 1910. (for shin-pads add rolled up newspapers).

Hockey is Canada's game. The game that Canada gave the world. The game that Canada is best known for.

The Best Hockey Game Ever Played Ever was played on Thursday 28 September 1972 in the Luzhniki Arena in Moscow between Canada and Russia (or as it was then the USSR). Canada and Russia don't have a lot in common, but two things they do have are cold weather and hockey.

In 1972 Canada and Russia played a series of eight hockey games against

A Bottle of Russian vodka. (not for export)

each other, the first four in Canada and the last four in Moscow. Quite incredibly not only was it the first time they had ever played each other, but it was the first time that Canada had ever put together a national team of its best hockey players.

Each country chose a team of 35 players. Canada chose 22 players from Ontario, 11 from Quebec and two from the Prairies. Of the 22 players from Ontario, seven were from Northern Ontario. Northern Ontario contributed 20% of the Canadian team and 32% of the players from Ontario, with 4% of the Ontario population. Northern Ontario makes hockey players.

There was one from Smooth Rock Falls, one from Kenora, two brothers from Schumacher, two brothers from Sault Ste. Marie and one from Kirkland Lake (he's on the plaque).

After the first four games in Canada, Russia lead the series two games to one with one tied. Then they won the first game in Russia. If Canada wanted to win the series it had to win the remaining three games in Moscow. Canada wins the next two games and the series is tied going into the last game.

On Thursday 28 September 1972 all of Canada comes to a stop in the afternoon to watch The Best Hockey Game Ever Played Ever. With 34 seconds left and the game tied 5-5 Canada scores the winning goal and wins the series. Of the six Canadian players on the ice when the winning goal is scored four come from Southern Ontario, one from Quebec and one from Northern Ontario. The winning goal is scored by Kincardine, Ontario assisted by Sault Ste. Marie, Ontario.

Hockey is Canada's game. And Northern Ontario makes more than its fair share of hockey players.

Chapter Seven

Timmins

The City of Timmins is made up of a string of once-separate towns (that are still basically separate), which stretch for 21 kilometres (13 miles) east-west along a highway: Timmins, Schumacher, South Porcupine, Porcupine.

Timmins is west of Schumacher, South Porcupine and Porcupine. Schumacher is east of Timmins, and west of South Porcupine and Porcupine. South Porcupine is west of Porcupine, east of Schumacher and Timmins and ever so slightly south of Porcupine. Porcupine is east of South Porcupine, Schumacher and Timmins and ever so slightly north of South Porcupine.

Timmins is gold. Gold makes people do crazy things. It made people go to the Yukon. It made people go to Swastika.

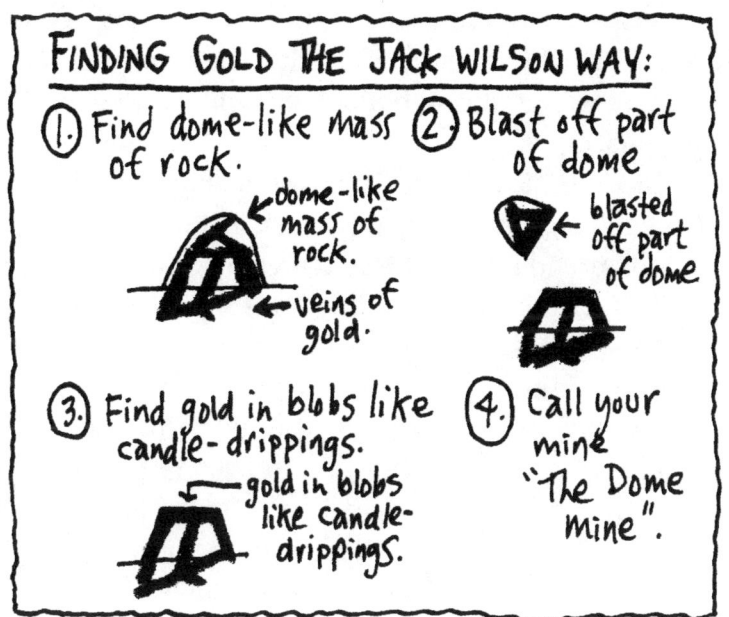

In 1909 it made Noah Timmins go to the Porcupine from Cobalt. In 1903 silver made Noah Timmins go to Cobalt from Mattawa, buy a ¼ share in a silver claim and strike it rich. So when the silver began to run out at Cobalt, gold made Noah Timmins go to the Porcupine.

But the story of Timmins does not start with Noah Timmins. It starts with prospectors. Prospectors look for minerals on the surface of the ground. Because of this they prefer the ground to be rock rather than grass. It makes things easier. Then they just scratch around a bit on the rock and if they find something interesting they stake a claim.

Reuben D'Aigle was a prospector from New Brunswick. He went to the Klondike, found gold in Alaska, took a two-week course in minerals at Queen's University, read a geologist's report on gold-bearing rocks in the Porcupine Lake area of Northern Ontario, and canoed in there from the west to take a look. There were plenty of rocks to scratch around on here. So he scratched around.

Just south of Gillies Lake (between Moneta Avenue and Algonquin Boulevard in modern-day Timmins), he dug some pits. There was gold here but not enough. So Reuben D'Aigle left the pits.

In 1909 Jack Wilson found some big dome-like masses of rock sticking up to the southwest of Porcupine Lake. He scratched around a bit and found a vein of gold. They blasted off part of the dome and found "gold in blobs like candle-drippings." It became the Dome Mine. It's still going today and you can visit it.

Benny Hollinger was a barber who also cut pulp wood but wanted to be a prospector. So in 1909 he and Alec Gillies (Gillies Lake) raised some money, went to the Porcupine, heard about the Big Dome find, went a little further west, found Reuben D'Aigle's pits, scratched around a bit, and found gold just lying there under the moss. "The quartz stood out about three feet out of the ground and was about six feet wide with gold splattered all over it for about sixty feet along the vein." It became the Hollinger Mine.

Sandy McIntyre and Hans Buttner heard Benny Hollinger and Alec Gillies whooping it up when they found gold, so they staked their own claims on the north side of Pearl Lake near to where Hollinger and Gillies had found gold. It became the McIntyre Mine.

Timmins had its three famous gold mines. Timmins has had over 200 mines, but these were the original three mines that built the town and kept it going.

Noah Timmins' nephew Al Pare worked at his uncle's silver mine in Cobalt. When they found gold in the Porcupine he rushed up there, saw the Hollinger and Gillies claim, rushed back to Cobalt and convinced Noah Timmins to buy the claims from Hollinger's uncle who as financial backer controlled the claims.

It was between the two uncles. Hollinger's uncle took the money and Benny Hollinger got a nice payout and a famous

FINDING GOLD THE BENNY HOLLINGER WAY:

1. Find Moss.
   ← moss
   ← gold

2. Lift Moss.
   ← moss
   ← gold

3. Find gold.
   ← gold

4. Jump up and down and whoop it up!

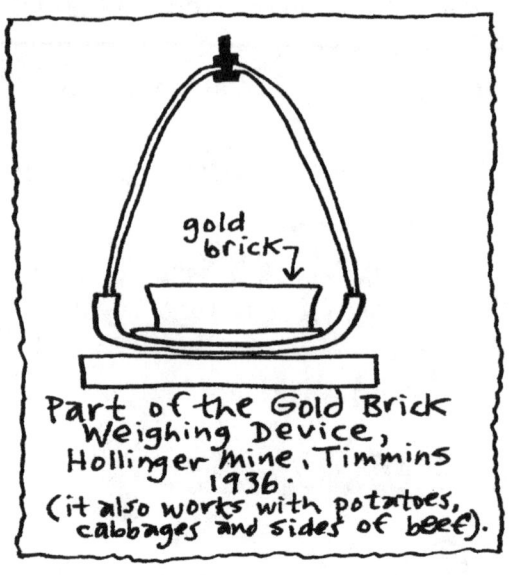

Part of the Gold Brick Weighing Device, Hollinger Mine, Timmins 1936. (it also works with potatoes, cabbages and sides of beef).

mine named after him. Al Pare's uncle bought the claims and the Timmins family became millionaires and had a town named after them. It was Al Pare who called the area Timmins after his uncle Noah. Over the next 58 years the Hollinger Mine produced over 19 million ounces of gold. You can visit it today as "The Timmins Underground Gold Mine Tour." The mine closed in 1968.

The McIntyre Mine didn't have the surface gold or strong ownership of the Dome and Hollinger mines, so it didn't get going until 1912. Hans Buttner sold his shares, went back to Germany, invested well and eventually settled in Kalamazoo,

An Early View of Part of the McIntyre Mine (about 5:15 a.m.)

A Late View of Part of the McIntyre Mine (about 11:30 p.m.)

Michigan, U.S.A. Sandy McIntyre sold his shares for $125, went down to Kirkland Lake, found gold again, sold those shares for peanuts as well and ended up with nothing. However the mine named after him kept going until 1988.

That was the unusual thing about Timmins. It was no fly-by-night, here-today-gone-tomorrow mining town. It didn't have spectacular ups and downs, booms and busts. It got up in 1910 and kept going.

Unlike most mining towns Timmins developed in a relatively orderly way. There was no mass migration and squatting all over the place. Things were much more manageable and civilized. When the first house was built in South Porcupine and later found to be located in the middle of the first street, the owner of the house happily moved it.

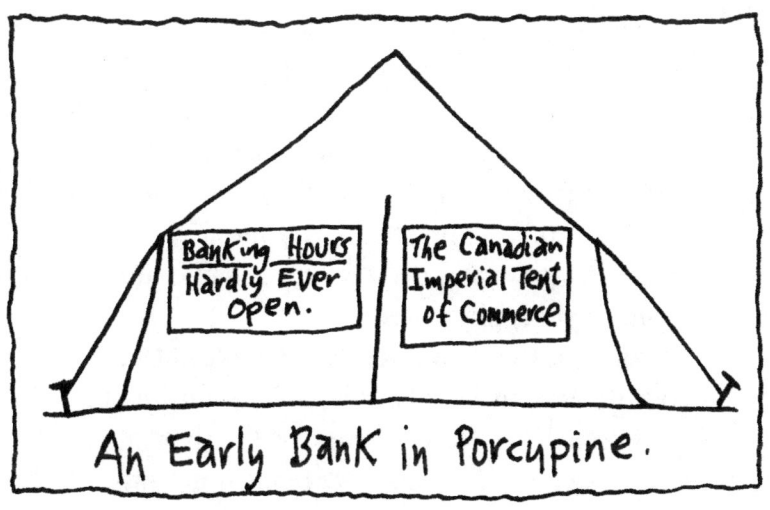

An Early Bank in Porcupine.

The first town in the "Porcupine camp" was Golden City (now part of Porcupine), at the east end of Porcupine Lake. This was because, other than Reuben D'Aigle who canoed in from the west, everybody else hiked into the Porcupine from the east (they called it a "camp" because in the beginning it was just tents and camping).

The next settlement was Pottsville (now also part of Porcupine), further west along the north shore of the lake. Then came South Porcupine at the south end of the lake, whose first street was named Golden Avenue even though it was one of the few places in the Porcupine where they found no gold.

The railway reached South Porcupine in 1911. And then just as things were getting nicely settled in -- FIRE! In the Porcupine if something wasn't rock or gold or lake, it was wood. The place was surrounded by trees and everything else was made of wood: wood roads, wood railway ties, wood buildings, wood bridges, wood tree stumps, cut wood, dead wood, firewood, wood piles.

Everything burned. Pottsville burned. South Porcupine burned. The mines burned. Only Golden City didn't burn. But the people of the Porcupine were used to fires and they had fire drills. They buried valuables in the ground. They put things in the lake. They put things in boats and put the boats in the lake. They stood in the lake. But the fire took everything anyway: mining records, 8,000 claim stakes and the lives of 73 people, including some who went down the Dome Mine (not part of the fire drill), and were asphyxiated.

The fire set the area back two years, but because of it Noah Timmins bought land and began selling lots in the new town of Timmins, with Third Avenue as the main street next to the railway. Because Timmins was starting from scratch, it soon overtook the towns around Porcupine Lake that had to both clean up and rebuild after the fire, and as a result it became the main town in the area (when cleaning up after the fire at the Dome Mine they retrieved $½ million in gold).

Fred Schumacher visited the Porcupine from the U.S.A. in 1912 and bought land near the Dome Mine and between the

Hollinger and McIntyre mines. Then he set up building lots in what would become the town of Schumacher, went back to the U.S.A. and sat on his land for 24 years until the Dome Mine bought him out (he kept doubling the price of every offer they made).

So you had South Porcupine and the Dome Mine, Schumacher and the McIntyre Mine, and Timmins and the Hollinger Mine. All very sensible and orderly. All they had to do now was to fill the place up with characters. There was Foghorn Macdonald, Texas Steve, Bacon Rind King, the White Rat (who ran a greenhouse that sold liquor), Caroline Maben Flower (the first woman prospector who wore elegant outfits and a holstered pistol) and Jack Dalton who ran the stagecoach line ("with push and perseverance we could always swear our way through").

Everything was going along nicely until 1963. Then two momentous things happened. First, five buses disappeared down a sink-hole at the old abandoned Moneta Mine, and then Timmins had its second big mining strike (the incidents were not related).

The Texas Gulf Company had detected an "anomaly" in muskeg 27 kilometres (17 miles) north of Timmins in 1959. They'd found hundreds of these "anomalies" in the Canadian Shield, but by 1963 were just getting around to taking a closer look at this particular one.

In mining an "anomaly" is any area showing a magnetic reading out of the ordinary. They find these areas using aerial electromagnetic equipment. Prospecting was getting pretty high-tech now. You didn't just scratch around on rock and lift moss any more. You prospected by aerial photography. It turned out to be the start of the Kidd Creek copper-zinc-silver mine, the largest single base-metal mine in the world.

The Hollinger Mine closed in 1968, but the Kidd Creek Mine opened in 1965. Timmins hardly skipped a beat. Steady mining is Timmins. Mines continue to open and exploration continues to go on around Timmins. There's still lots of rock to scratch around on and photograph.

The Mine Head Frame Telephone Booth Timmins

The most interesting tourist attraction in Timmins? Why gold mining; what else? You wouldn't go to Niagara Falls and miss the falls, would you? Timmins has got the Underground Gold Mine Tour of the old Hollinger Mine. It's got old abandoned mines you can drive around and look at. It's got tours of a working sawmill and a working mine. It's got the Timmins Museum which specializes in things gold mining. And it's got local jewellers who specialize in things gold.

It takes 116,667 parts rock to find one part gold. Find enough one parts over a long period of time and you've got yourself a Timmins. Easier said than done. That's why there's only one of them.

The Front Part of The Polar Bear Express Just Pulling Into Moosonee.

CHAPTER EIGHT

The Polar Bear Express

The railway opened up Northern Ontario before roads did. It should come as no surprise then that Northern Ontario has two railway trips for railway enthusiasts. Railway trips with a difference. There's the Algoma Central Railway from Sault Ste. Marie to Hearst and the Polar Bear Express from Cochrane to Moosonee.

When they built the railway north from North Bay discovering gold, silver and farm land along the way, it didn't reach Moosonee until 1932. And there it stopped. On the west bank of the Moose River. Seventeen and a half kilometres (11 miles) south of James Bay. Two hundred and ninety-eight kilometres (186 miles) north of Cochrane. One thousand and sixty-nine kilometres (668 miles) north of Toronto. End of the line. All out.

There are only four ways to reach Moosonee from the south: fly, canoe, hike or take the Polar Bear Express Railway. At one time however the main way to reach Moosonee was not up from the south at all, but down from the north. Down through Hudson Bay and James Bay and up the Moose River.

And the destination was not Moosonee either, but an island in the river across from Moosonee.

A Canadian trivia question: If Kingston, Ontario is the oldest continuous settlement in Ontario and Kingston was first settled by the French, what is the oldest settlement in Ontario first settled by the English?

Not many people would guess that the answer lies on that island in the Moose River: Moose Factory. The Hudson's Bay Company established a fur-trading post at Moose Factory in 1673. But why did the English come into Ontario first from the north? Because it was easier. And because the French were in the south.

The Georgian Bay Indians told the French fur traders that the real source of furs was the Cree Indians who lived near "The Bay of the North." It was they who were "the best huntsmen in all America." If you could find "The Bay of the North" you could find the real source of furs.

Two French fur traders, Radisson and Groseilliers wanted to find this "Bay of the North," but the French king would not listen to them. But the English king would. So in 1668 the English put Radisson in a ship called the "Eaglet" and Groseilliers in a ship called the "Nonsuch," and sent them off to find "The Bay of the North" and "to trade with the Indyans there," and "to have in yor thoughts the discovery of the Passage into the South Sea" (they were still trying to find a western short-cut to China). The Eaglet had to turn back, but the Nonsuch kept going finally stopping at the mouth of

The Nonsuch 1668.
beam: 15 feet, length: 53 feet
(replica now moored in Winnipeg)

the Rupert River on James Bay (now Rupert House, Quebec). Here they built a log cabin and spent the winter. In the spring 300 Cree Indians came to them with furs to trade. They loaded up the Nonsuch with furs and returned to England in 1669. Mission accomplished (except they didn't find the Passage).

What a success! Get in a ship. Sail over. Dock. Trade. Fill the ship with furs. Sail back. Sell the furs for a profit. No canoes. No voyageurs. No long portages. Only one voyage to the real source of furs. Couldn't be easier. And so the Hudson's Bay Company was formed in London, England in 1670. The English would now come into Canada from the north, the back door, and take the fur trade from the French.

In 1672 they sent three more ships into James Bay and built fur-trading posts at Fort Albany (Albany River), Charlton Island and Moose Factory. The Hudson's Bay Company had started the exploration and settlement of Hudson Bay and James Bay which would make this part of Northern Ontario at one time more important than Southern Ontario, and certainly a much more important part of Canada than it is today. For a time James Bay was as much a front door into Canada as the St. Lawrence River was.

Little did they know however that they'd already discovered this "Bay of the North" before. Captain Thomas James was in James Bay in 1631, and Henry Hudson was in Hudson Bay in 1611. But James never knew about furs and we never knew what Hudson thought because he was put adrift in a small boat by a mutinous crew and never seen again.

The fur trade, Hudson Bay and James Bay were important for more than 200 years. And then they were no longer important. They went back to being "north" again. Back to being isolated. Back to being the back door. But the Cree Indians of course just carried on. Today the populations of Moosonee and Moose Factory are 85% Cree Indian, descendants of those "best huntsmen in all America."

The Polar Bear Express leaves Cochrane in the morning and arrives in Moosonee in the early afternoon. On the trip north the scenery passes through the Northern Ontario claybelt (most northerly agricultural area in Ontario), across the Moose and Abitibi rivers, through forests of slow-growing 200-year-old black spruce and across muskeg.

The train has a dining car, snack car, special events for kids, tour guide presentations and a children's hour in the entertainment car on the way back.

If you're not in any hurry to get back you can go to a hunting and fishing camp, look for Beluga whales in James Bay, look for fossils on Fossil Island, look for birds on the Shipsands Island Waterfowl Sanctuary, take a hike on muskeg, or camp on Tidewater Provincial Park Island.

If you're on the day trip you have about five hours before the train leaves again. Either way you have time to cross the Moose River to Moose Factory by ferry, freighter canoe, ice road (winter), or helicopter (spring breakup, fall freezeup) and to visit the fur trade museums in both towns.

Most of the tourists come in the summer, but the railway is not just for tourists. Ontario Northland Railway also run the "Little Bear" train, three days a week, all year round, returning between Cochrane and Moosonee the next day. It's a mixed freight/passenger train, and one of the last "flag-stop" train services still left in Canada, stopping to pick up or put down anywhere along the line it's requested.

The Polar Bear Express. A train trip back to the days of the fur trade. A train trip through a little part of the vastness and isolation of Canada that not many Canadians see. A train trip to "The Bay of the North."

Chapter Nine

Sudbury

What do you think of when you first think of Sudbury? That Sudbury was the first city in Canada to install parking meters? (1940, so the next time you can't find a coin for a parking meter you know who to blame). That Sudbury's Lake Ramsey is the largest lake in any city in North America? That Sudbury had the first municipally-owned and operated electrical system in Ontario? (1896). That Sudbury's underground Neutrino Observatory is the most advanced neutrino detector for sub-atomic research in the world?

A Sudbury Parking Meter (courtesy: Sudbury Parking Meter Museum and Hall of Fame).

If you said any of the above you would be correct. But Sudbury is more than that. It also has the world's tallest smokestack (1,250 feet); the world's tallest nickel coin (30 feet); and a very fine Science Centre where you can pet a porcupine, a snake or a butterfly (choice of 600); ride a flight simulator; explore space; visit a robotics lab; test canoe paddles; go down a nickel mine; lie on a bed of nails; make a soapstone carving, a hurricane or a snowstorm; and see the biting parts of a mosquito up close.

Sudbury is also the biggest city in Northern Ontario. The biggest city between Manitoba and Quebec north of Georgian Bay. The biggest city in an area the size of 1¾ Yukons.

But being the biggest city in Northern Ontario doesn't

mean everything. It doesn't mean that much to Kenora for instance. Kenora is 1,461 road kilometres (913 miles) away from Sudbury. It's hard to be chummy when you're 913 road miles and one time zone away. Yet they're both in Northern Ontario. Being the biggest city in Northern Ontario does have its limits. The vastness of Northern Ontario does that to you.

Sudbury is only where it is because when the Canadian Pacific Railway was being built, they measured out stations every so many miles and Sudbury just happened to be one of those every so many miles that they measured out a station to (1883).

The CPR moved 3,350 railway workers into Sudbury and a railway official named it Sudbury after his wife's birthplace in England. But nobody thought Sudbury would be around long. It was just a temporary railway construction town. After all, who would want to live here permanently? There was nothing here but rocks, trees, lakes and swamps. And there was nothing special about rocks, trees, lakes and swamps. Just about everywhere in Northern Ontario had rocks, trees, lakes and swamps to spare.

But as it turned out Sudbury had something else to spare too. Copper and nickel. Not as exciting as silver and gold perhaps, but well worthwhile going after anyway. By 1885 though the railway workers had gone and there were only a few hundred residents left (the ones who quite liked the local rocks, trees, lakes and swamps).

Then Sam Ritchie, an American from Ohio, came to town. Ritchie saw some Sudbury ore samples in the CPR offices in Montreal, formed the Canadian Copper Company of Cleveland, Ohio with a branch plant in Copper Cliff (now part of Sudbury), and sent an ore sample away to be analysed (1886).

All this mining activity attracted people to come to Sudbury other than to catch the train. The Ontario government sent surveyors, and the CPR drew up the first town plan (1886) with the railway lines and railway yard as the focal point of the town (naturally), and a grid pattern of roads and lots that paid no attention to the rocks, trees, lakes and swamps running out from that.

Cedar Street Public School 1890. The First School in Sudbury. Built with cedar logs. Wherever possible schools built on streets named after trees were built with logs from those trees.

North-south streets were named after people (Lorne, Elgin, Durham, Lisgar), and east-west streets were named after trees (Fir, Beech, Elm, Cedar, Larch). Elm was the main street, and Durham and Elm was the main corner. The remnants of this first town plan can still be seen in Sudbury today.

Then the results of the Sudbury ore analysis came back. The good news was that not only was this one of the greatest deposits of copper in the world, but the ore also contained nickel. The bad news was that nobody knew what to do with nickel.

The first thing you need to know about nickel is how to spell it. Nickel rhymes with "pickle," "prickle," "fickle" and "tickle." But it's the only "ickle" word spelt "el" and not "le." As a result a lot of people misspell nickel.

Nickel is an odd-ball word. But then nickel is an odd-ball metal. Nickel is a silvery-white metal which resists corrosion, has a high strength over a wide temperature range, and looks nice when you polish it. First discovered in 1751, the name nickel comes from the old Saxon word "kupfernickel" (coppernickel) which meant "mischievous devil" because the old Saxon miners found nickel ores were a devil to mine (they didn't know what to do with nickel either). Even today the process of extracting nickel from its ore is a complex one.

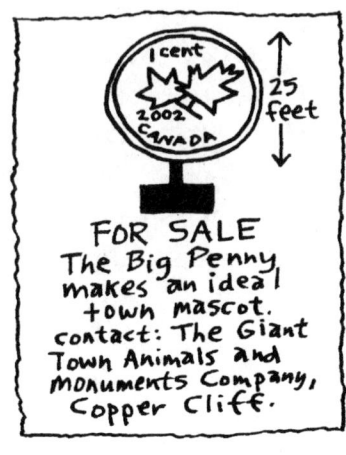

FOR SALE
The Big Penny makes an ideal town mascot.
contact: The Giant Town Animals and Monuments Company, Copper Cliff.

There are only a few metals which exist naturally in their pure state: gold, silver, copper and platinum being the best known. All the others, like nickel, exist mixed up in rock. The only way to get them out is to melt them out.

Nickel is only the 24th most common metal in the earth, so when they found it at Sudbury it was a mixed blessing. Sure, it was nice to find, but they still had the same old problem as the Saxons, how to get it out of the rock (and economically); and once they had got it out, what to do with it? Who would buy nickel and what would they use it for?

The answer came in 1889 when research in Europe showed that an alloy of nickel-steel was the best material for making armour-plating for ships. Nickel had a use! (In the 1950s the American defence department considered nickel "the world's most critical material.")

A Chunk of Crystaline Copper Found in a Cliff near Sudbury.

Ritchie went to see the American navy. Nickel had a buyer! So Copper Cliff developed the first economical process to smelt (melt) nickel from ore.

The Copper Cliff Method of Nickel Extraction 1889

1) Dig the ore out of the ground.
2) Crush the ore into two sizes: fine and coarse.
3) Take the ore to roasting yards with roasting beds (ground covered with clay and gravel).
4) Spread a layer of fine ore on the roasting bed to a depth of 6 inches.
5) Put a layer of wood over this to a depth of 18 inches (this is why they originally cut down a lot of trees around Sudbury).
6) Cover the wood pile with a layer of coarse ore to a depth of 2-3 feet.
7) Cover with another layer of fine ore.
8) Set fire to the pile.
9) Burn for 4-7 weeks. The sulphur in the ore will keep the fire going. It will also over time, as they found out, kill vegetation (this is another reason why for a long time Sudbury didn't have many trees).
10) At the end of the burn take the roasted ore to a smelter furnace, add coking coal, and set fire to it again (or blast it).
11) Draw off the heavier molten metal, cool it, and send it to a refinery (the first nickel refinery in Canada was at Port Colborne, Ontario).
12) Take the remaining "slag" from the smelter and dump it in a slag heap between Copper Cliff and Sudbury.
13) Get ready for the booms and busts of being a mining town.

Actually as mining town boom and busts go, Sudbury has had more booms than busts. Otherwise it wouldn't have grown up to become the biggest city in Northern Ontario, would it?

Boom: 1890s, three mines.

Bust: Price of nickel goes down, town becomes "dull," businessmen play quoits.

Boom: The Spanish-American War (1898), Canadian Copper expands, Mond Nickel arrives, traffic is so busy the town passes a bylaw requiring all vehicles to drive on the right-hand side of the road (1913), WW1 starts.

Bust: The Sudbury Horticultural Society cancels its inaugural flower show "because most of the plants in town have been severely injured by sulphur fumes" (1912), WW1 ends and there is no peacetime use for nickel.

Boom: The Canadian mint invents the five-cent nickel coin (1924), new uses are found for nickel (cars).

Bust: There is only one nickel company left, Mond and Canadian Copper merge to form INCO (International Nickel Company of Canada) 1928, they find coal near Chelmsford, but it won't burn.

Boom: Falconbridge Nickel arrives, INCO builds a 510-foot-tall smokestack (1929) in the hope that "the hot fumes escaping into the rarer atmosphere 500 feet from the surface of the earth will be disseminated to such a degree as to nullify the injurious effects they would have on the vegetation of the area," (the Sudbury Horticultural Society is not convinced).

A Sudbury Quoit (nickel-plated) — 10-12 inches

Small Bust: The Depression lasts only two years in Sudbury.
Boom: WW2.
Small Bust: WW2 ends.
Boom: Demand for stainless steel (8-10% nickel), INCO builds a 636.5-foot-tall smokestack (1956), (the Sudbury Horticultural Society remains sceptical).
Bust: The world turns to industrial plastics and nickel is discovered in other countries.
Boom: INCO builds the "Superstack," 1,250 feet tall, the tallest smokestack in the world (1971), Sudbury starts a very successful grass- and tree-planting program (1978), (the Sudbury Horticultural Society rejoices!)

Today nickel is still a devil of a metal to extract from its ore. But there are now a lot more things that it can be used for. It's mixed with other metals to form over 3,000 different alloys for use in some 250,000 different things.

At one time Canada was the world's largest nickel producer and Sudbury was the nickel capital of the world. Today Russia produces more nickel and Canada mines nickel in Labrador, Manitoba and Alberta as well as Sudbury. But Sudbury is still the spiritual home of nickel. Where nickel first started out on its way into 3,000 different alloys and 250,000 different things.

*****

If you look at a map of Sudbury today you will notice that it's a rather spread out city. There are a number of perfectly good reasons for this. Sudbury started out life as a railway town planned by a railway company who wouldn't let anybody else build within one mile of its railway station (not a good policy for attracting commuters).

The Jesuits also owned land in Sudbury, so you couldn't build there. Then the mines came along and built their own mining camps, later towns: Copper Cliff, Falconbridge, Lively, Creighton, Frood Mine; so you couldn't build there. Then there were the rocks, trees, lakes and swamps which determined where you couldn't build. And then there were the early Sudbury people who were of the independent type, quite happy not to have any more restrictions about where they couldn't build and quite content to allow themselves to build wherever they wanted to build. So they did. After all there was still lots of room. Even after the railway, Jesuits, mines, rocks, trees,

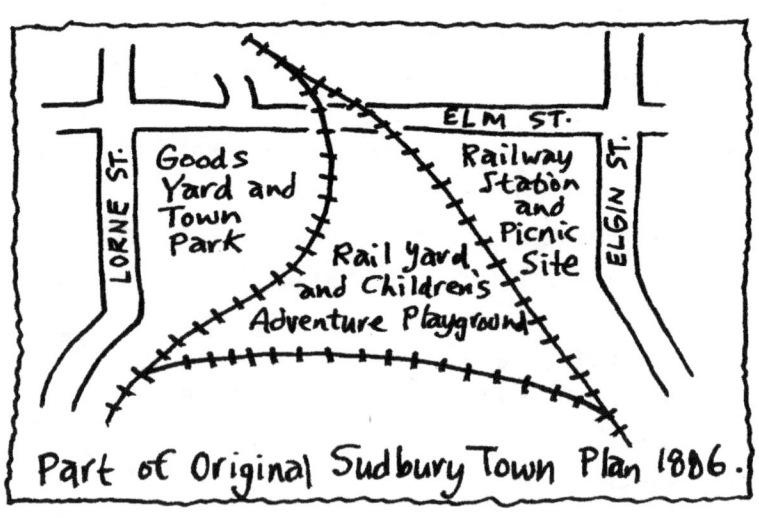

lakes and swamps had told them where they couldn't build. The last thing they needed was themselves telling themselves where they couldn't build as well. So they didn't do it.

Sudbury had no town planning until 1955. In 1930 an alderman talked about it, but it was only idle talk by one alderman. In 1940 they appointed a Town Planning Commission, but their only accomplishment was the installation of the famous downtown parking meters. In 1947 they formed some planning areas and published a planning report recommending some planning initiatives, but nothing else happened. However in 1955 they hired their first planner for their first planning department and Sudbury was off and planning. The results however of following an earlier unplanned existence were perhaps better than they would have been if the town had continued with the rigid grid pattern first started by the railway (see Kenora chapter).

The first shopping mall arrived in Sudbury in 1957. This meant that the people could finally escape from the downtown parking meters. The second shopping mall arrived in 1981, but by that time they had also done a lot of re-building in the downtown to try to offset the damage done by the parking meters (parking meters turned out to be not all they were initially cracked up to be).

And so Sudbury turned itself around. It re-grew its trees and it re-planned itself. The result was Northern Ontario's biggest city. And you only get to be the biggest by having more people who want to live there. More people who quite like the local rocks, trees, lakes and swamps.

* * * * *

The Sudbury Basin is a large basin-like depression in the ground north of Sudbury, 59 kilometres (37 miles) long by 27 kilometres (17 miles) wide. Some people believe that two million years ago a huge meteorite hit the earth here causing the basin and lots of valuable minerals and farm land to be formed.

Other people believe that the basin, minerals and farm land were caused by a huge volcanic eruption. Still other people believe that they were caused by a combination of the two (meteor followed by eruption, or eruption followed by meteor).

A few people (but not many), believe that the Sudbury Basin was formed by a large giant (probably the same one that

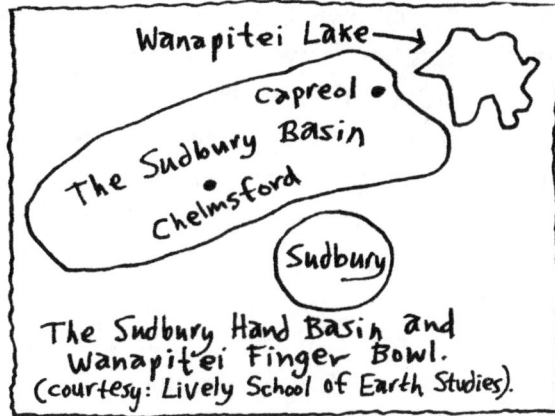

The Sudbury Hand Basin and Wanapitei Finger Bowl.
(courtesy: Lively School of Earth Studies).

fell asleep near Thunder Bay), scooping out the earth to make a basin to fill with water in order to wash its face and hands.

This idea is scoffed at however by the meteor and eruption believers who say, "Why would a giant scoop out a hand-basin when all he had to do was use Wanapitei Lake which was right nearby?"

The giant believers however say, "Wanapitei Lake wasn't big enough for a hand basin, and was in fact actually used as a finger bowl."

Anyway, nobody really knows how the Sudbury Basin came to be. They just know that it's basin-shaped and good for minerals and farm land.

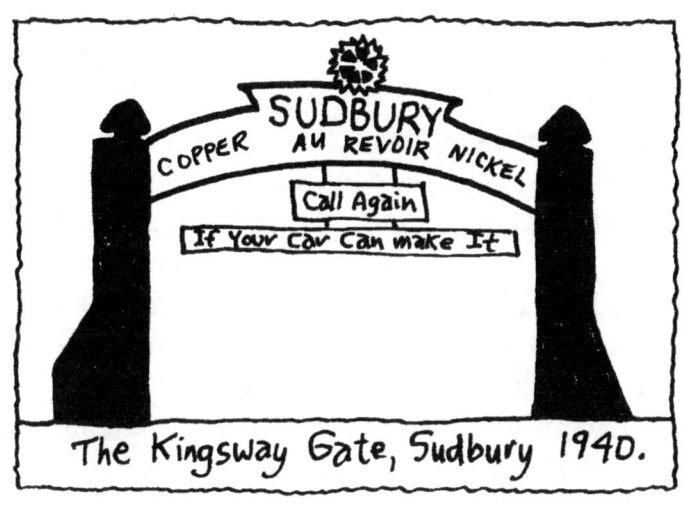

The Kingsway Gate, Sudbury 1940.

Chapter Ten

The Colossal Rise, Rather Big Fall, and Gradual Rise Again of Elliot Lake

Elliot Lake is a mining town that went from a population of zero and no mining companies, to a population of 25,000 and 12 mining companies in four years; then lost 18,400 people and 10 mining companies in seven years; and then gradually gained people back again despite ending up with no mining companies left at all.

Elliot Lake is not your average mining town. In fact Elliot Lake isn't a mining town any more. Elliot Lake is a former mining town that's now the biggest town of any type between Sudbury and Sault Ste. Marie. And in Northern Ontario that's really saying something.

A chunk of uraninite in pitchblende embedded in feldspar. (courtesy: Elliot Lake Uranium Souvenir Gift Shop).

Chapter One: The Colossal Rise

The story of Elliot Lake begins in 1931 when a rock sample sits in the Mining Recorder's Office in Sault Ste. Marie. It sits there until 1949 when a local hotel owner and amateur prospector with a Geiger counter, gets a radioactive reading from it. The rock sample comes from Long Township, 21 kilometres (13 miles) east of Blind River between Algoma Mills and Spragge.

The hotel owner hires a former paper mill worker and amateur prospector also with a Geiger counter, to search the mining claims records of Long Township looking for uranium finds. After weeks of searching the former paper mill worker and amateur prospector gives up, takes his Geiger counter north of Lake Superior to prospect for uranium, and meets a professional geologist also prospecting for uranium. The former paper mill worker tells the geologist about the rock sample in Sault Ste. Marie. The geologist is interested.

Uranium is a hard silvery-white metal identified in 1789 and discovered to have radioactive properties in 1896, which can be used to make a nuclear reaction, including nuclear power and a nuclear reaction in a nuclear bomb.

In 1950 the Cold War is on. People were digging bomb shelters and stocking them with sleeping bags and tins of beans. Because of the strategic importance of uranium, the Government of Canada controlled the sale of Canadian uranium through its company Eldorado Mining and Refining. The main buyer of uranium was the United States Atomic Energy Commission, who were buying all the uranium they could get. Find uranium and you had a guaranteed buyer. So that is why the hotel owner, the former paper mill worker and the geologist were all looking for uranium.

One day the hotel owner and the former paper mill worker found an old prospecting pit in Long Township that made their Geiger counters click. They staked and registered their claim and collected rock samples. But the samples contained only a trace of uranium. The hotel owner and the former paper mill worker were puzzled. So they took the geologist to the pit too. The geologist is also puzzled, but secretly he has a rock sample tested. Maybe the radioactivity is caused by thorium? But only a trace of thorium is found. What is causing the Geiger counters to click?

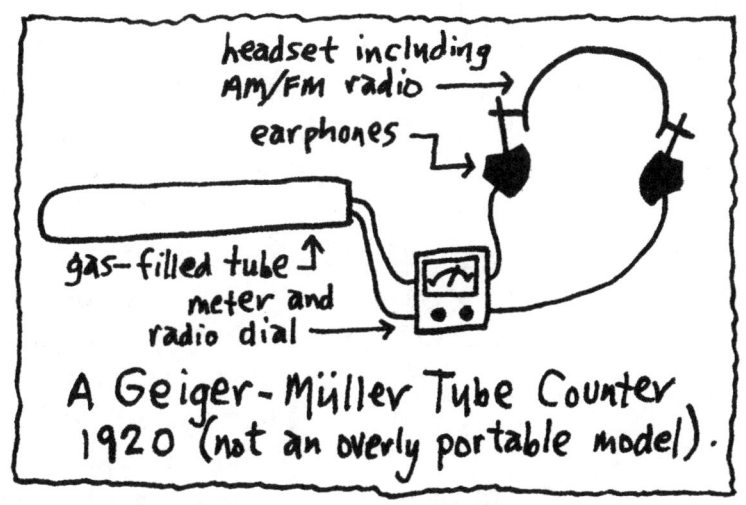

A Geiger-Müller Tube Counter 1920 (not an overly portable model).

The geologist tells a rich mine owner from Timmins via New York about the rock sample. Secretly the geologist and the rich mine owner wait for the claims of the hotel owner and the former paper mill worker to expire. Then they re-stake the area for themselves. It is now 1952. But they still don't know why the rock sample has such a low uranium rating. Then in 1953 the geologist is reading an article on uranium and finds out: "On exposure to the atmosphere uranium minerals oxidize and the surface uranium is completely leached out, with the result that practically no trace of uranium can be detected on the outcrop of even the richest uranium-bearing conglomerates."

With only a month to go before their claims also expire, the geologist and the rich mine owner drill down into the old prospecting pit and send an underground rock sample for analysis. The results: uranium. Secretly they stake more claims in Long Township.

But how much uranium is there and where is it? They find an old 1922 Geological Survey of Canada map. It shows that the same uranium-bearing geological features in Long

Township stretch for 144 kilometres (90 miles) in a big "Z" formation north of Lake Huron. The rich mine owner sends out teams with Geiger counters to investigate. The results: uranium. But would they be able to stake the whole 144-kilometre-long "Z" before registering their claims within 30 days of staking as required?

The rich mine owner has a plan. It would become known as "The Back Door Staking Bee." They leave Long Township. Everybody would think they had gone. But they would sneak in from the north (the back door) with an army of stakers hired from Timmins and stake the whole "Z." Everything was secret. Military precision. Mining licences were obtained from different mining offices. The stakers were not told where they were going. They flew off in float planes on a roundabout route, landed on lakes, set up camps, and began staking according to instructions. Each staker could register 18 forty-acre claims, nine in Sudbury and nine in the Sault (the area overlapped two mining districts). The staker's ownerships would then be transferred to the rich mine owner. Nobody would know they were there. They staked 1,600 claims. But they were spotted before they were finished, and when they registered their claims, news of "The Back Door Staking Bee" is out and there is an Algoma Uranium-Staking Rush.

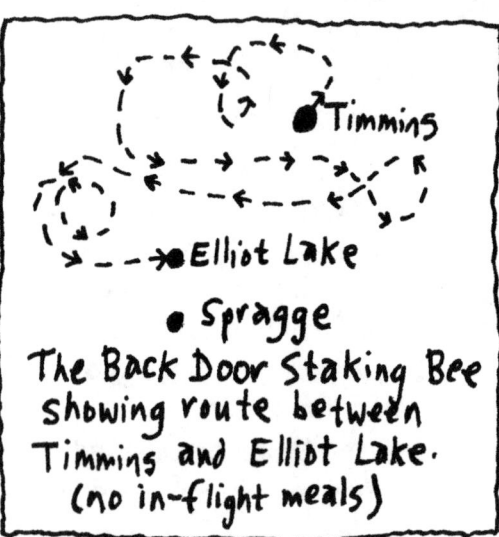

The Back Door Staking Bee showing route between Timmins and Elliot Lake. (no in-flight meals)

The rich mine owner forms Algom Uranium Mines (the name was supposed to be "Algoma" but when the name was registered the last "a" was somehow missing). The first mine is the Pronto Mine in Long Township near Spragge. It was now 1954. The Pronto Mine was close to the main highway, but the other mines needed roads into the bush. And where would everybody live?

A new townsite was needed. Algom Mines suggested a site near Elliot Lake, one of a string of lakes in the middle of the "Z." The province approved the site. It is now almost 1955.

Elliot Lake would be a mining town with a difference. Usually each mine built its own self-contained temporary settlement. But Elliot Lake would be a permanent town to serve all the mines. The rich mine owner wants to build a "New City" near the Pronto Mine with a swimming beach, library, office building, apartments, houses, shopping mall, concert hall, arena and art gallery (the rich mine owner collected art).

The federal government sets a deadline for uranium contracts. Twelve mines meet the deadline, seven controlled by the rich mine owner and worth $497 million out of over $1 billion in contracts running from 1956-1962.

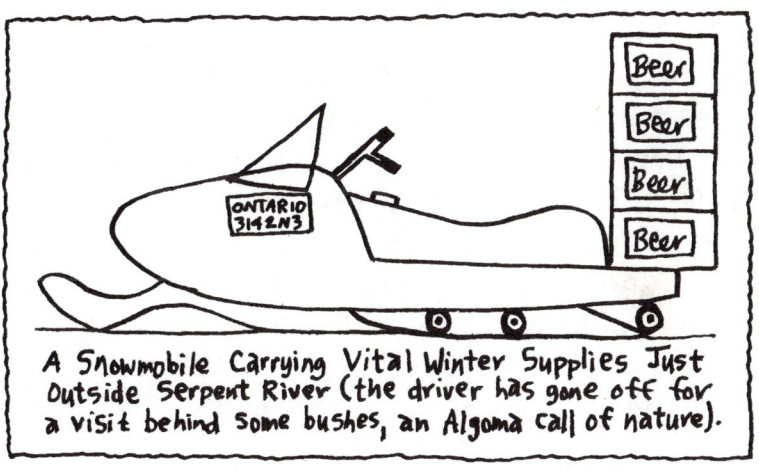

A Snowmobile Carrying Vital Winter Supplies Just Outside Serpent River (the driver has gone off for a visit behind some bushes, an Algoma call of nature).

Elliot Lake grows loosely following a plan amended as they go along. Lots are surveyed as requested. There was a school, butcher, gas station, cafeteria, movie theatre, pool hall, 25 permanent houses and bunkhouses, mobile homes, tents, trailers, shacks and mud everywhere. But no "New City." And even the rich mine owner does not have the money to develop all his mines. There was just too much uranium at Elliot Lake.

It was now 1956. The rich mine owner sells out to Rio Tinto Mines becoming an even richer former mine owner. He goes on to live in New York, the Riviera and Toronto. The geologist also sells out. He was now a rich millionaire geologist. And so the rich mine owner and the geologist leave the Elliot Lake story. The town later names a street after each of them (there are no streets named after the hotel owner and the former paper mill worker).

It was now 1957. Elliot Lake builds roads, 1,300 houses and water and sewer lines through the winter, rock, dysentery and infectious hepatitis. There are 13,556 people living in and around Elliot Lake, and an unknown number of squatters not counted in the census. There was a temporary municipal building, police shack and jail. Commercial lots sold by auction sell out. It was homesteading. It was pioneering. It was a town growing up too fast for itself. People who moved to Elliot Lake in 1957 were "newcomers." Those there since 1956, "oldtimers." Those there since 1955, "living legends."

It was now 1958. There are 188 businesses, 2,700 telephones, 25,000 people, 2,000 mobile homes, 14 churches and paved roads. But the library, post office, police, fire hall and municipal offices were all in shacks. The court room was in the theatre (the Bench was a wooden bench made of planks), and there were 41 deaths: 4 by natural causes, 4 murders, 3 traffic fatalities, 1 drowning, 1 burning and 28 killed at the mines. Elliot Lake was a wild and woolly place.

Chapter Two: The Rather Big Fall 1959-1966

1959. Three mines close. There is too much uranium. The U.S.A. will not buy any more Canadian uranium. Uranium is found in the U.S.A., France, South Africa and Australia. World demand was 50,000 tons/year, supply 1.5 million tons. The former paper mill worker drowns while canoeing.

1960. One hundred and thirty-five women from Elliot Lake dress in white sheets to represent ghosts and go to Ottawa to demand that the government save their town from becoming "the world's most modern ghost town." Four more mines close.

An Elliot Lake Ghost in Ottawa 1960. (there are 134 others too)

1961. Another mine closes. Two hotels close, the town offices move into one and a nuclear museum moves into the other. Plans for a new post office are reduced from a two-storey building to a one-storey building costing $20,000 more. An empty house becomes a funeral home. An empty apartment building becomes a Centre for Continuing Education. The Elliot Lake drinking water is radioactive. Fish die in local rivers and lakes. A new Provincial Park, School of Fine Arts and Mine Research Laboratory open. Population falls to 6,600. Per capita municipal debt is the highest in Ontario. Central Mortgage and Housing owns half of the Elliot Lake housing, most of it empty.

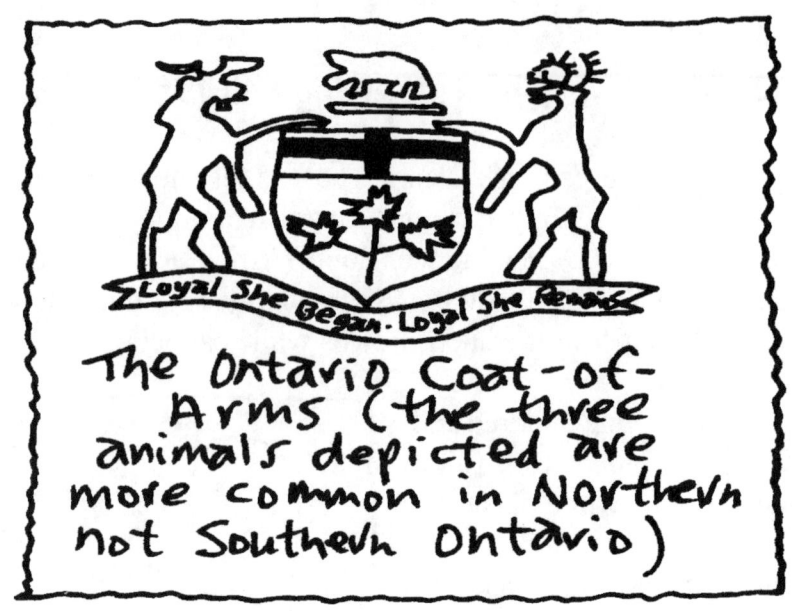

The Ontario Coat-of-Arms (the three animals depicted are more common in Northern not Southern Ontario)

Chapter Three: The Gradual Rise Again 1967 -

The market for uranium improves. There is a housing shortage again. The funeral home moves to another empty house because the house it is in is sold. A new church, school, airport runway and Nursing Assistants Training Centre open. One mine closes but one mine and one hotel re-open. The Elliot Lake rink gets walls and a roof.

The market for uranium slumps. The library moves into another empty building now owned by the town due to unpaid taxes. The police station moves out of the empty school into an empty hotel, and the School Board moves into the empty school.

Elliot Lake holds its first "Uranium Festival" (1971), to raise money for a municipal building, and passes its first "Official Plan." The town dump moves. One mine closes and a new one opens. The town installs a lawn sprinkler system that never works, and gets a swimming pool that leaks with a leaky roof. The hotel owner drowns while fishing (1973).

The market for uranium improves. Two mines re-open. Canada is the only country with uranium for sale. A shopping mall, 39 new businesses, two new hotels, a funeral home and more houses are built. The Elliot Lake Airport has new washrooms but no water.

The market for uranium slumps. A U.S.A. contract is cancelled. A mine will not re-open. Plans for a new sewage treatment plant are reduced from a big one to a small one costing $250,000 more. There are 1,000 empty houses. Elliot Lake first starts to attract retired people to live in the empty houses and to promote tourism (1988). The Mine Research Laboratory, Kresge's and the Nursing Assistants leave Elliot Lake. Two re-opened mines close. Elliot Lake discusses 26 different projects to save the town in 26 different rooms. The even richer former mine owner opens an art gallery in Washington, D.C. The town sells 170 houses for $1 million worth of TV advertising on a TV fishing show. The fishing show sells 170 Elliot Lake houses on its fishing show shown in 30 countries. Germans cannot believe you can buy a house in a beautiful area that looks like their Black Forest for such a low price. The last uranium mine in Elliot Lake closes (1996).

A Thick Slice of Black Forest Cake.

A Thick Slice of Elliot Lake Provincial Park Cake.

(baking courtesy of Elliot Lake Bavarian and Algoma Specialty Bakery, Brunet Road, Elliot Lake)

But Elliot Lake doesn't care any more. It no longer lives or dies with the ups and downs of uranium. It has six other things going for it now: fresh air, elbow room, attractive Black Forest scenery, peace and quiet, cheap housing, and lots of get-up-and-go-people who are not getting-up-and-going from Elliot Lake.

It also has hunting, fishing, hiking, camping, canoeing, boating, cross-country skiing, skiing skiing, mountain biking, swimming, rock climbing, snowmobiling, golfing, skating, curling, basket-weaving and jolly retirement living; as well as an Academy of the Arts, Nuclear and Mining Museum, Canadian Mining Hall of Fame, and an Historical Society.

Elliot Lake isn't a mining town any more. It's a former mining town. And the biggest town between Sudbury and Sault Ste. Marie. Of any type.

Cast of characters

The hotel owner:	*Aimé Brèton*
The former paper mill worker:	*Karl Gunterman*
The geologist:	*Franc Joubin*
The rich mine owner:	*Joseph Hirshhorn*

The man who prepared the 1922 Geological Survey of Canada map of the big "Z" formation and has a hall in Elliot Lake named after him: *W. H. Collins*

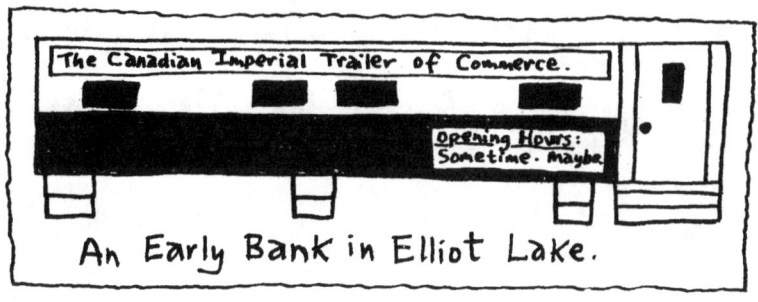

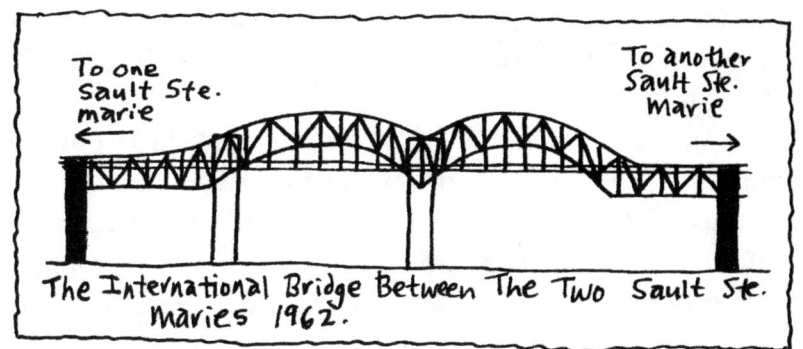

The International Bridge Between The Two Sault Ste. Maries 1962.

CHAPTER ELEVEN

Sault Ste. Marie

Sault Ste. Marie is the sort of town that took a long time to decide what it wanted to be when it grew up. So it tried a lot of different things along the way.

But before Sault Ste. Marie ever got started doing anything, it had something to think about that no other town in Canada did. It had a twin city across the river in another country. Its twin city had the same name it did. Its twin city spelt its name the same way it did. And people continually had trouble spelling both their names properly.

There are only two sets of twin cities along the whole of the Canada/U.S.A. border that have the same names spelt the same way: Niagara Falls, Ontario and Niagara Falls, New York; and Sault Ste. Marie, Ontario and Sault Ste. Marie, Michigan.

Sault Ste Marie, Michigan was first settled in 1668. Sault Ste. Marie, Ontario never got going until 1796. Sault Ste. Marie, Michigan is the third-oldest city in the U.S.A. Not a lot of Americans know that. Not a lot of Americans think about Sault Ste. Marie, Michigan. To Americans Sault Ste. Marie, Michigan is somewhere away up there in the back of beyond.

At the end of civilization as they know it. The further south you go from Sault Ste. Marie, Michigan, the smaller Sault Ste. Marie, Michigan gets.

But at Sault Ste. Marie, Ontario, Canada is only just beginning. The further north, west or east you go from Sault Ste. Marie, Ontario, the bigger Sault Ste. Marie, Ontario gets. Sault Ste. Marie, Ontario is the biggest place between Sudbury and Thunder Bay (989 kilometres, 618 miles). Sault Ste. Marie is the biggest place in the southwestern corner of the southwestern quarter of the northeastern half of Northern Ontario. And that's saying something (Northern Ontario is over six times bigger than the whole state of Michigan, including the top bit).

Ever since French fur traders found rapids in the St. Marys River, the two Sault Ste. Maries have had a problem with spelling. The Indians called this place "Bawating" which meant "place of mighty rapids," or "water pitching over rocks." Quite a nice name really and very appropriate. But not French enough for the French. So they called it "Sault de Gaston" instead.

"Sault" means either "jump," "rapids" or "waterfall." Whatever it means it's difficult to spell, which is why some people (the poor spellers), have taken to spelling it "Soo" (the easy way out).

After Sault de Gaston they called it "Sault de Sainte Marie" or "Ste. Marie de Sault." Finally they settled on "Sault Ste. Marie" (the other rejected choices were: "Sault Marie Ste.," "Ste. Sault Marie," "Marie Sault Ste." and "Marie Ste. Sault").

This meant that not only did you have to remember how to spell "Sault," but you had to remember that it was "Ste." not "Saint" or "St.," "Marie" not "Mary," and that there were no hyphens anywhere.

Sault Ste. Marie was lucky that it had the chance to try different jobs as it was growing up. Lots of other towns never

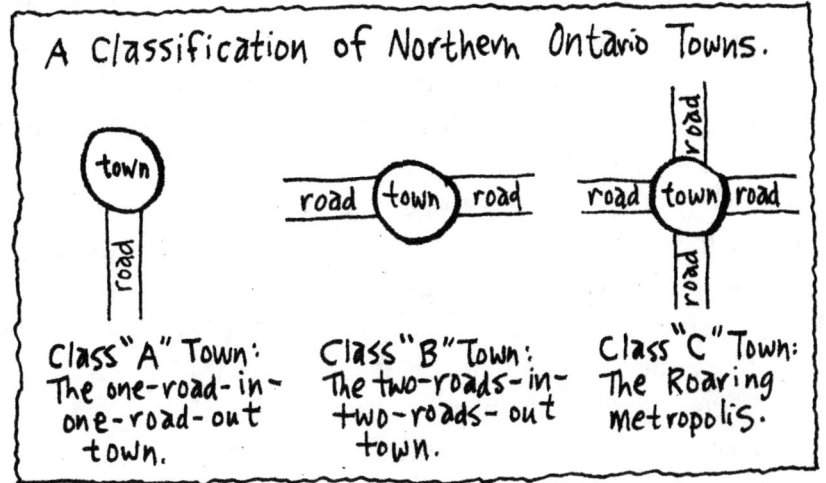

had a choice. They were told at an early age what they were going to be. Especially Northern Ontario towns. They were told: "You're going to be a mining town," or "You're going to be a pulp and paper town," or "You're a little dot on the landscape equidistant between two other little dots on the landscape, and the train comes by every once in a while, and there'll be a road along sometime, and Toronto's away down there, and the best thing you can do is to just get on with it and make your own fun." So they did. (There's a lot of little dots on the landscape making their own fun in Northern Ontario).

    The people of Sault Ste. Marie never had any fear about going to Toronto though, despite the fact that it's 688 modern road kilometres (430 miles) away. In 1832 Chief Shingwaukonce snow-shoed to Toronto to ask for a school teacher. One was sent. In 1871 his son walked to Toronto to ask for a school. One was built. In 1896 a town delegation went to Toronto to ask for a hospital. No money was given. In 1935 a town delegation went to Toronto to ask for better roads. The Trans-Canada Highway arrived 33 years later.

All the early activity at Sault Ste. Marie was on the American side. The Canadian side was too low and swampy to bother about. But after the American Revolution (1796), the British had to leave the south side of the river and move to the north side and bother about it.

They built Fort St. Joseph and the first canal on the river (a canoe lock, 1798). Sault Ste. Marie was now a fur trade port. But during the War of 1812 the Americans came across and destroyed both the fort and the canal, and by 1821 the fur trade was gone altogether, so that was it for the fur trade.

Basically though the two Saults learned early on that their best friend was each other. When a temporary colonel at Fort Brady on the American side fired cannonballs across at the Canadian side (1866, no damage), the other American officers came over and apologized once the temporary colonel had left.

The Canadian Sault used the American Sault's post office. Before 1863 the only way to mail a letter in Canada from Sault Ste. Marie was to paddle down Lake Huron to Sandwich (Windsor, Ontario), and mail it from there. After that, in order for the post offices to tell the two Saults apart, the American Sault adopted zip code 49783, while the Canadian Sault adopted postal code P6A followed by a number, a letter, and another number. But as far as jobs went, Sault Ste. Marie still had to find something else to do.

The Indians had found copper at Bawating, but there was not enough of it. Sault Ste. Marie was not going to be a mining town. Lumbering came to the north shore of Lake Huron, but Sault Ste. Marie was not at the centre of it. Sault Ste. Marie was not going to be a lumbering town. Farming was not so hot either. Sault Ste. Marie had struck out at fur trading, mining, lumbering and farming.

So why not try government administration? In 1858 the "Judicial District of Algoma" was formed and they began appointing people to fill the new government positions. They were not always easy to fill. Sault Ste. Marie was called "a wild and horrid and inhospitable place, I should not like to live there," by the first Algoma District judge who eventually did live there seven years after his first visit.

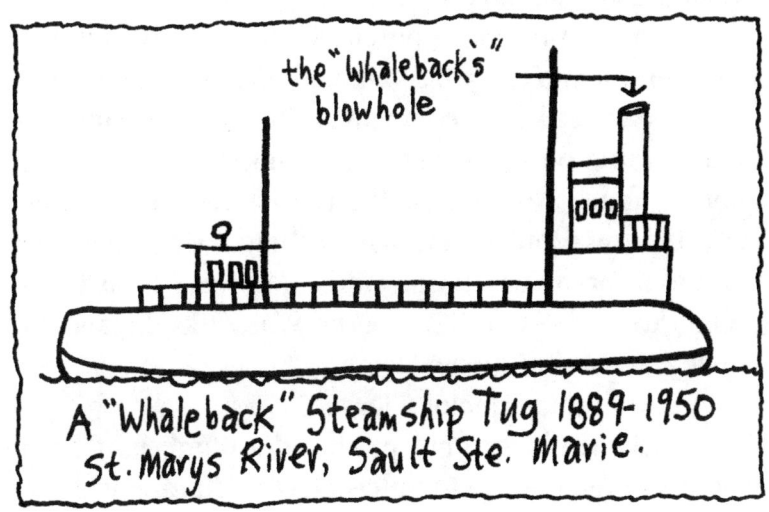

However Sault Ste. Marie's main occupation continued to be as a water link between the two lakes. But they still couldn't get through the rapids. So the Americans built their first canal in 1855 (in 1840 the American Secretary of State said that "a canal at the Sault would be almost as useful as a canal on the moon"). They shared it with Canada until 1870 when they refused permission for its use to a Canadian military expedition to the Red River Rebellion. (They later relented). As a result Canada built its own canal (1895). By 1979 though the Canadian canal was no longer part of the St. Lawrence Seaway, and commercial traffic on both sides used the American canal. But Sault Ste. Marie had found a full-time job as a Seaway town. You can take a tour of the canal and locks today.

The year 1887 was an important one for Sault Ste. Marie. The railway arrived, it became a town, and the Sault Ste. Marie Water, Gas and Light Company was formed to use the rapids for hydro-electric power. Sault Ste. Marie would become a horizontal Niagara Falls! But the power company purchased some land and then ran out of money.

It changed its name, purchased more land, and then ran out of money again (they'd spent it all on land). The town then became a partner in the company. They raised more money, started building on all the land they'd bought, and then ran out of money again. By the time the power canal was completed (1894), the town owned the whole thing. But when they let water into it for the first time a wall collapsed. It was fixed, but the Ontario and Sault Ste. Marie Water, Light and Power Company was out of money again.

Enter Francis Hector Clergue.

Northern Ontario has produced a number of colourful characters in its time, and Francis Hector Clergue is definitely one of them. Clergue spent only nine years in Sault Ste. Marie. But what a nine years they were!

The Nine Years of Francis Hector Clergue 1894-1903

The Clergue Blockhouse 1894.
Huron St, Sault Ste. Marie.

Francis Hector Clergue of Bangor, Maine, U.S.A. heard about the exciting business opportunities in hydro-electric power in Sault Ste. Marie, Ontario. Francis Hector Clergue was very good at hearing about exciting business opportunities, and talking other people out of their money to invest in them. Unfortunately he was not that good at making them successful. He was an exciting business opportunities failure.

He'd failed with streetcars, tourism, dry docks, banks and a railway across Persia before he came to Sault Ste. Marie and bought the power company. Sault Ste. Marie's nine-year ride with Francis Hector Clergue had begun. One thing just led to another . . .

The power plant was finished, but there was nobody to buy the power. So Clergue built a pulp mill. But nobody would buy liquid pulp that had to be shipped so far. So Clergue built a foundry to make the machinery to dry the pulp, and Sault Ste. Marie became the first place in the world to produce dry pulp.

But chemical processing with sulphur would improve the quality of the dry pulp. So Clergue bought a nickel mine in Sudbury to get the sulphur ore to process the pulp. But the residue from burning sulphur ore was a nickel-iron metal that somebody wanted to buy. And the sulphur ore also had copper in it which could be removed by putting it in salt water and passing an electric current through it. So Clergue bought salt. But copper refining also produced chlorine. So Clergue built a plant to use the chlorine to bleach the wood pulp.

But having done all that the nickel-iron metal still had too much nickel in it. But iron ore could be used to dilute the nickel. There was iron ore at Wawa that they'd found when they'd been looking for gold. So Clergue bought an old gold mine at Wawa to get the iron ore to produce the nickel-iron metal from the sulphur ore.

But the iron ore at Wawa was 224 kilometres (140 miles) north of Sault Ste. Marie. So Clergue built the Algoma Central Railway and bought a fleet of eight freight steamers, five barges, three passenger steamers and a tug to bring the iron ore

The Barnes Block 1902 Queen St. East Sault Ste. Marie (note mortar and pestle on top).

to the Sault. But rather than use the iron ore to make metal for somebody else to make into steel, why not make the steel yourself? So Francis Hector Clergue formed the Algoma Steel Company and built a steel plant (1902).

* * * * *

Algoma. It's hard to talk about Sault Ste. Marie without mentioning the word "Algoma." The word pops up all the time. Algoma is actually a made-up word. A word made up by an American, Henry Rowe Schoolcraft (1793-1864), as a new name for Lake Superior (even though it didn't really need one). The "Al" stands for "Algonquin," and the "goma" is Algonquin for "waters." There is a Schoolcraft County in Upper Michigan, but for some reason the word Algoma was picked up and used more in Canada than it ever was in the U.S.A.

* * * * *

To everything else, Clergue added: a water system; streetcars; veneer mill; railway car shops; plants to make bricks, charcoal, acetate of lime and wood alcohol; a ferry service between the two Saults; and a hotel and boarding house.

The population of Sault Ste. Marie tripled to keep pace with all the exciting business opportunities. But Francis Hector

Clergue was running out of other people's money. Just nine years after coming to Sault Ste. Marie, Francis Hector Clergue was forced to resign. It was another exciting business opportunities failure. But a spectacular one at that. And in the long run not a total failure either.

Remnants of the nine years of Francis Hector Clergue remain in Sault Ste. Marie today: Algoma Steel, Algoma Central Railway, Great Lakes Power, and St. Marys Paper all got their start with Francis Hector Clergue. And you can visit Clergue's Powerhouse and Superintendent's Residence, and the house he built using the old North West Company powder magazine called the Clergue Blockhouse (1894) too.

Francis Hector Clergue moved from Sault Ste. Marie to Montreal where he died in 1939. But before then he had more exciting business opportunity failures in Canada, the U.S.A., Russia and the Far East. But none were as spectacular or as long-lasting as in Sault Ste. Marie, Ontario.

* * * * *

After Francis Hector Clergue things settled down a bit in Sault Ste. Marie. They could hardly get more exciting. Clergue was a hard act to follow. Nobody ever has yet.

Because of all the trees and forest fires around Sault Ste. Marie, the Ontario Air Service was started in 1924 to fly in fire-fighting crews to remote areas. It's now the world's largest fleet of fire-fighting planes. Because of all the bushplanes flying around, the Canadian Bushplane Museum was opened in Sault Ste. Marie as well.

The Canadian Sault gradually overtook and became bigger than the American Sault, but the people of the two Saults continued to be best friends. They smuggled liquor across the river to each other. They worked and went to school on both sides. They held the annual "Great Tugboat Race," and the annual "Bridge Walk and Trot," two miles across the International Bridge. (If you want to walk further you can walk on the Voyageur Trail, part of the Trans-Canada Trail, either east to Elliot Lake (200 kilometres/125 miles), or north to Victoria, B.C., via Inuvik and the Yukon (10,829 kilometres/6,768 miles).

The two Saults even share each other's holidays and fireworks. On July 1, Canada Day, everybody gathers on the American side to watch the fireworks on the Canadian side from across the river. On July 4, Independence Day, everybody gathers on the Canadian side to watch the fireworks on the American side from across the river.

Sault Ste. Marie. A town that's done a lot of different things and is always on the lookout for other different things to do. After all, you never know when another Francis Hector Clergue might come along. Sault Ste. Marie. More than just a pretty name that hardly anybody can spell properly.

The Former Sault Ste. Marie Howling Wolf and Two Evergreens Farewell Archway on the Highway east of town.

CHAPTER TWELVE

The Group of Seven

The Group of Seven were a group of seven Canadian painters. Artist painters, not house painters. There were actually more than seven of them too. Altogether there were ten of them, but they would probably best be called The Group of Seven Plus One.

They weren't all born in Canada either. Four were, three weren't, and the Plus One was. The four came from Montreal, Toronto, Brantford and Orillia; the three came from England; and the Plus One came from Owen Sound, Ontario.

The Group of Seven are best known for painting Canadian landscapes and being the first to establish a unique Canadian identity and style of art. And the landscapes they are best known for painting are not the landscapes of Toronto, Montreal, Brantford, Orillia and Owen Sound, but the landscapes of Northern Ontario.

Prior to the Group of Seven Plus One, Canadian painters copied European painters, and painted picnics at Niagara Falls, lambs in fields, and certainly no winter scenes (they discouraged immigration). "Art in Canada meant a cow or a windmill. They were grey, mild, inoffensive things, and when surrounded by heavy gold frames, covered with plate glass, and had a spotlight placed over them, they looked expensive." (A. Y. Jackson, Montreal, one of the seven).

However when the Group of Seven Plus One came along they changed all that. They painted the rugged scenery of "The North," the rocks, trees, lakes, rivers, sunsets, sky, shores and leaves. Their paintings had such titles as: "Terre Sauvage," "Snow in October," and "Frost-laden Cedars." The Group of Seven Plus One didn't give a hoot about immigration.

A Hasty Sketch From Distant Memory of the painting "The Edge of the Maple Woods" by A.Y. Jackson 1910. (the first painting Jackson ever sold).

In 1911 A. Y. Jackson exhibited his paintings in Toronto. J. E. H. MacDonald (England, one of the seven), Tom Thomson (Owen Sound, the Plus One), Lauren Harris (Brantford, one of the seven, the rich one), and Arthur Lismer (England, one of the seven) liked his paintings and Harris (the only one with money), bought one which showed an old barn, split rail fence and trees with no leaves on them. It was the first painting A. Y. Jackson had ever sold.

Two years later Jackson hadn't sold any more paintings, and went to Toronto. There he met MacDonald, Thomson, Harris, Lismer, Frederick Varley (England, one of the seven), Franklin Carmichael (Orillia, one of the seven), and Frank Johnson (Toronto, one of the seven) and became the eighth member of The Group of Seven Plus One. The painters were all in place. Now all they needed was their canvas.

In 1913 Harris and MacDonald saw an exhibition of Scandinavian art, were impressed by the landscapes which looked a lot like Canada, and reached the conclusion that the future of Canadian art lay not in flower arrangements and sheep, but in the landscapes of "The North" and that their group were going to paint it. So they did.

The first areas they painted were Georgian Bay and Algonquin Park. Then World War I came along and the group dispersed. Jackson and Varley painted the war for the Canadian War Records Commission. The others went off to war too. But Thomson drowned while canoeing in Algonquin Park. So when the Group of Seven Plus One reassembled after the war, there were only seven of them now, not eight. The Plus One was gone.

In 1918 they went looking for new scenery to paint, and took the Algoma Central Railway north from Sault Ste. Marie. They liked what they saw, especially the Agawa River Canyon, Batchawana Rapids and Montreal Falls, all still on the route today of the Algoma Central Railway. So they arranged with the railway to lend them a caboose to use as a painting studio (Francis Hector Clergue's contribution to Canadian art).

It was not until 1920 however that the group decided to hold their own exhibitions and adopt the name The Group of Seven, and not until the British Empire Exhibition in England in 1924 that The Group gained real recognition. The British press called them: "The new school of landscape painting." They had just not painted Canada in a new way, they had created a whole new way of painting.

Back in Canada the nice critics said: "Their daring colours have brought vitality to Canadian art, which a few years ago showed only signs of senility." But the not-so-nice critics called them: "The Hot Mush School of Art, more like a glob of porridge than a work of art. If the Canadian section of the British Empire Exhibition is to be covered with crude cartoons of the Canadian wilds, we should advise the Department of Immigration and Colonization to intervene."

Immigration again! An awful lot of people spent an awful lot of time back then worrying about Canadian immigration. But it didn't worry The Group of Seven. They

"I'll Put Them In Water"
A typical flower arrangement painting poo-pooed by The Group of Seven Plus One.

pushed on further north and painted the Rossport, Jackfish, Coldwell and Pic Island areas of the north shore of Lake Superior.

In 1927 Emily Carr came to meet them, and because of this resumed painting again after a break of 15 years, returning to British Columbia to become one of Canada's most famous artists.

The last Group of Seven exhibition was in 1931. The next year they disbanded. They were no longer the rebels-against-the-establishment painters they had been. They were now the establishment.

And so in the way of things the next generation of Canadian painters turned away from the landscapes of the Group of Seven and went back to painting urban things again. But that too is typical. Canada is a country of two parts: urban, the small part; and everywhere else, the big part. The group of Seven Plus One knew that. That's why they painted the big part.

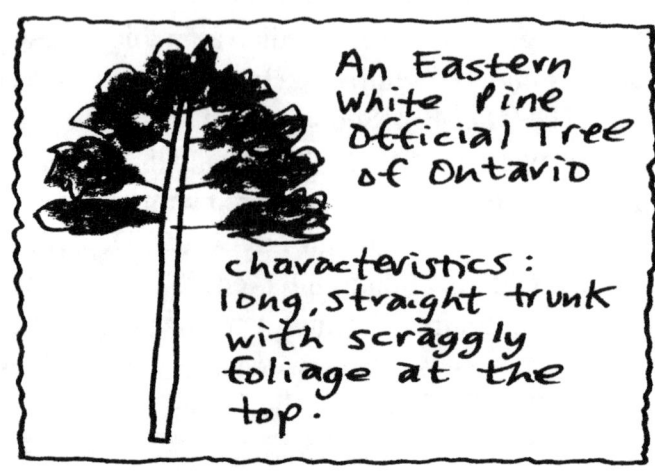

An Eastern White Pine Official Tree of Ontario

characteristics: long, straight trunk with scraggly foliage at the top.

CHAPTER THIRTEEN

The Algoma Central Railway

When the Group of Seven landscape painters were looking for some scenery to paint, they had the whole of Northern Ontario to choose from. They chose the scenery along the Algoma Central Railway line from Sault Ste. Marie north to Hearst. They especially liked the area around the Agawa Canyon, Montreal Falls and Batchawana River. The Algoma Central Railway still goes there.

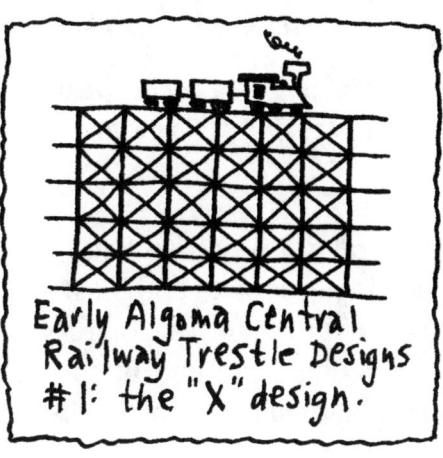

Early Algoma Central Railway Trestle Designs #1: the "X" design.

Like the Polar Bear Express, the Algoma Central Railway was not originally built for tourism, and is not entirely a tourism railway. It just turned out that way. Tourists and painters enjoyed the trip, and tourism helped to keep the trains going.

The Algoma Central Railway was built by Hector Francis Clergue in 1899 to bring iron ore from Wawa south to the Algoma steel plant in Sault Ste. Marie. By 1906 the railway had been built further north and connected with the main east-west Canadian Pacific Railway line at Franz. Eight years later it reached the main east-west Canadian National Railway line at Oba and the town of Hearst. Where it stopped. End of the line. All out.

Like a lot of railways though it wasn't always smooth tracking for the Algoma Central. It went into debt once and had three financial reorganizations before it reached Hearst, and

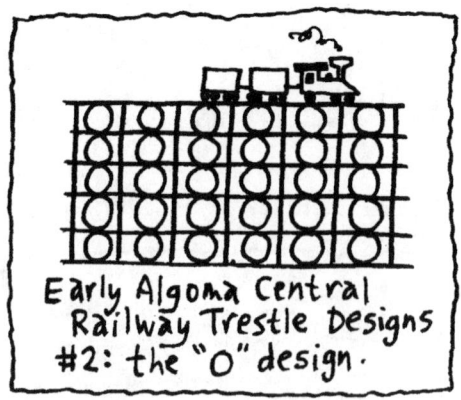

Early Algoma Central Railway Trestle Designs #2: the "O" design.

didn't entirely climb out of the red until 1959. Today the railway not only hauls freight and tourists, but owns forestry reserves and property as well. There's more than one way to run a railway.

The tour of the whole 474 kilometres (296 miles) of the Algoma Central Railway from Sault Ste. Marie to Hearst, takes two days and includes an overnight stop in Hearst. Whereas the end of the line of the Polar Bear Express is Moosonee, a mainly Cree Indian community, the end of the line of the Algoma Central is in Hearst, a mainly French-speaking community. Northern Ontario is different.

The 182-kilometre (114 miles) Agawa Canyon day trip leaves Sault Ste. Marie in the morning and returns in late afternoon. It's a day in the office of the wilderness of Northern Ontario. The trip includes a two-hour stopover in the canyon itself.

Early Algoma Central Railway Trestle Designs #3: the "X's and O's" design.

A popular time to take the Algoma Central Railway is in late September/early October, the colour season, when the leaves are coloured red, orange, green and gold. Or you can take The Snow Train in the winter, the white season, when everything is coloured various shades of white.

Chapter Fourteen
Wawa

Northern Ontario has a wide variety of place names. It has some colourful place names: Silver Dollar, White River, Black Hawk, Red Lake, Golden Valley and Vermilion Bay. It has some musical-sounding place names: Attawapiskat, Couchiching, Kakabeka Falls, Batchawana Bay. It has some place names which make you pause before attempting to pronounce them: Wunnummin Lake, Kashechewan, Opasatika, Biscotasing. It has some places that sound like law firms: Rayside-Balfour, Markstay-Warren, Starratt-Olsen, Chaput Hughes. It has some place names which are just fun to say: Moonbeam, Pickle Lake, Shining Tree, Summer Beaver. And it has some place names which are just plain unusual: Central Patricia, Arbor-Vitae, Oxdrift, Jaffray Melick, Eaton-Rugby. And Wawa.

The Giant Goose of Wawa (related to The Giant Muskie of Kenora, The Giant Moose of Dryden and The Giant Nickel of Sudbury).

Wawa is also a short place name. But it's not the shortest place name in Northern Ontario. Oba and Emo are shorter. But

Wawa is still a pretty short place name. But for a short name it had a long story to get there.

A Speckled or Brook Trout Awaiting a Fishing Hook near Lochalsh (requires hardly any bait).

Wawa's original name was Michipicoten, which is quite a nice name itself. They looked for gold here but found more iron ore instead. It was from an old gold mine at Wawa that Francis Hector Clergue got the iron ore for the Algoma Steel plant in Sault Ste. Marie.

You would think that with such a short name as Wawa they wouldn't have had any difficulty in spelling it. Well they did. Their first spelling in 1899 was "Wa-Wa." Then in 1933 they changed it to "Wawa." But in 1951 they changed it completely to "Jamestown," in honour of Sir James Dunn, a president of Algoma Steel after Francis Hector Clergue.

When Sir James Dunn died in 1959, the town observed a respectable and appropriate period of mourning, and then changed their name back to Wawa again in 1960. There were too many Jamestowns in the world anyway. But there couldn't be too many Wawas. Especially ones with a 28-foot-tall metal Canada goose with a 19-foot wingspan at its town entrance.

Wawa means "wild goose." Michipicoten means "great bluff." It's easier to put up a statue of a goose than a bluff. And much more interesting to put up a statue of a goose than one of Sir James Dunn.

The section of the Trans-Canada Highway that passes by Wawa and its giant goose, was one of the most difficult sections of the highway to build, and was not completely finished until 1960.

Chapter Fifteen

Black Bear White River

This is the true story of a soldier, a town, a bear, a zoo and a book; and how they all became connected.

August 1914. The First World War is on and Captain Harry Colebourn, a veterinarian from Winnipeg, Manitoba, is on a train heading east with the Fort Garry Horse Regiment. The train stops at White River in Northern Ontario; an area of rocks, trees, lakes, rivers, small towns, not many roads, and lots of wildlife, including Black bears. While the train is stopped Captain Colebourn buys a small Black bear cub for $20. Not unusual. Orphan bear cubs were often found around White River and sold as pets. He takes the bear on the train with him and names her "Winnipeg," or "Winnie" for short.

When Captain Colebourn's regiment goes overseas to England, Winnie goes along too. She lands at Plymouth, is stationed on Salisbury Plain, sleeps under Captain Colebourn's cot, follows soldiers around like a dog, and becomes the mascot of the Second Canadian Infantry Brigade. But when the brigade is posted to France in December 1914, Winnie cannot go along, so Captain Colebourn loans her to the London Zoo. Not unusual. During the war four other bear cubs would also end up at the zoo.

When the war is over Captain Colebourn returns to the zoo to get his bear. But she has become such a popular attraction that he decides to leave her there. Children love Winnie. She is the only bear considered completely trustworthy by the zoo. Children ride on her back and she eats from their hands. So Captain Colebourn returns to Winnipeg where he retires in 1945 and dies two years later at the age of 60 after falling down some stairs at home.

A Honey Jar Similar to the One Owned by Winnie-the-Pooh.

Which is when the connection between a soldier, a town, a bear and a zoo comes to an end; and the connection between a town, a bear, a zoo and a book begins.

Alan Alexander Milne takes his son Christopher Robin to the London Zoo to see his favourite animal, Winnie. A. A. Milne is a writer. One day he writes a children's story about a bear and a boy. The boy is named Christopher Robin. He changes the bear from a girl bear to a boy bear, but keeps the name Winnie. In 1926 the story becomes a book called "Winnie-the-Pooh."

Meanwhile the town called White River has taken to calling itself "The Coldest Place In Canada." In 1936 it was -50°C/-72°F in White River. But then the record is broken by Moosonee and lots of other places (it's currently held by Snag, Yukon, -63°C/-81°F, 1947). So as White River could no longer call itself "The Coldest Place In Canada," and as there was really no sense in just sitting around to see if they could become the coldest place again, they decided to call themselves "The Birthplace of Winnie-the-Pooh" instead. So they did. And every year on the third weekend in August they hold a "Winnie Hometown Festival," which is a whole lot better than holding a "Coldest Place In Canada Festival" sometime in January.

The bear named Winnie lived in the London Zoo for 20 years and died in 1934. She was the best bear the zoo ever had. There is a statue of her there, and one of Captain Colebourn too; and there are also two plaques, one with some wrong information on it, and another presented to the zoo by school children from White River in 1997.

And that is the true story of how the soldier, the town, the bear, the zoo and the book all became connected.

Chapter Sixteen
Black Flies

The Right Wing of a Black Fly (pulled off by a canoeist in Lake Abitibi)

The moose is the official symbol of Northern Ontario. The call of the moose. The call of the North. But the moose is not the most common animal in Northern Ontario. Not by a long shot. There is another much smaller animal which is much more common and makes much less noise. The black fly. The black fly is the unofficial symbol of Northern Ontario (Northern Ontario has mosquitoes too, but the mosquito is the unofficial symbol of Manitoba).

Northern Ontario is well known for its black flies. The Canadian Department of Immigration doesn't like people talking about black flies of course, but then no place on earth's a complete paradise is it? They have stinging jellyfish in Australia and sharks in Florida and people still go there don't they? Northern Ontario isn't just contented canoeists canoeing, fun-loving fishermen fishing, and happy hikers hiking. It's canoeists, fishermen and hikers swatting black flies too. Black flies may be the black side of life in Northern Ontario, but you can't sweep them under the carpet, can you? (On the bright side there are no stinging jellyfish or sharks in Northern Ontario).

Black flies live anywhere there is moving water. And they especially like northern wooded areas. So you can see why they prefer to live in Northern Ontario so much.

It wouldn't be so bad though if black flies were just black and flew around like other flies. But they don't. They bite as well. But only the females bite, and only out of a need for self-preservation. They need blood for egg development. They're not fussy where they get this blood; they'll bite anything with blood in it. If they had a choice they'd probably prefer to bite cattle since cattle can't swat back. But Northern Ontario has a shortage of cattle, so they bite canoeists, fishermen and hikers instead. (They bite moose too, but moose have a black fly antidote. They submerge themselves in water).

But it's not all black news about black flies. The good news is they only live for three weeks and they're only .06 inches long. And Canada leads the world in the battle against black flies. A company in Trout Creek, Ontario (south of North Bay), invented a complete set of clothing which will keep black flies off you. Sort of like wearing a portable mosquito net. And the University of Western Ontario in London, Ontario developed a special solution applied with an electro-magnetic gizmo, which helps keep black flies off animals.

But other than that you'll just have to learn to live with black flies like the people of Northern Ontario do. Keep your tent flaps shut, and if they get too bad do what the moose do. And be thankful that the waters of Northern Ontario contain no stinging jellyfish or sharks, because they're a whole lot worse than black flies.

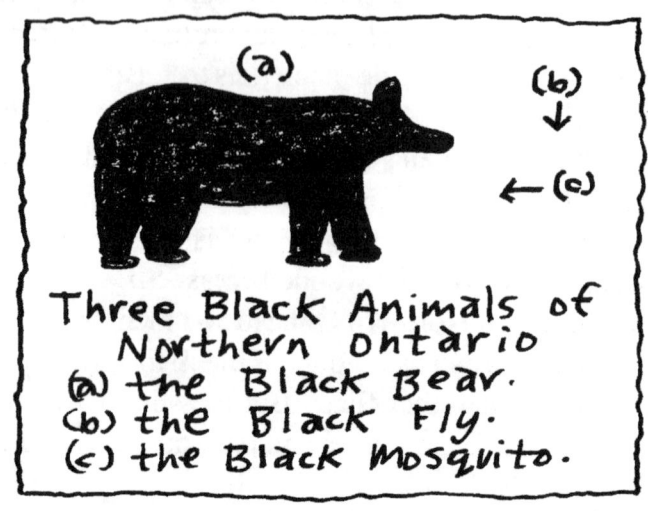

Three Black Animals of Northern Ontario
(a) the Black Bear.
(b) the Black Fly.
(c) the Black Mosquito.

CHAPTER SEVENTEEN

Parks

As the number of people in Ontario gets less the farther north you go, the number of parks gets greater. And camping, hiking, canoeing, outdoor wilderness parks these are too; not strolling, sitting, park-bench-swings-and-slides parks.

The Trans-Canada Highway south branch almost follows the shoreline of Lake Superior from Sault Ste. Marie to Thunder Bay. The whole 712 kilometres (445 miles) is dotted with parks. National parks and Provincial parks. Big parks: Pukaskwa (Ontario's largest National Park, coastal hiking trail, canoe routes), Lake Superior (scenic shoreline); medium-sized parks: Middle Falls, Sleeping Giant, Steele River; and smaller parks: Batchawana Bay, Pancake Bay, Obatanga, White Lake, Neys, Rainbow Falls, Ouimet Canyon (3 kilometres, [2 miles] long, 350 feet deep, 500 feet across), Kakabeka Falls (the Niagara of the north). A park every 54 kilometres (34 miles). And that's not counting private and municipal campgrounds either. A trail of parks.

Northern Ontario is loaded with lakes. So it's loaded with lake parks too. The Lake of the Woods has four provincial parks around it. Quetico Provincial Park is a canoeing park of lakes bigger than Prince Edward Island with 1,488 kilometres (930 miles) of canoe routes and 2,000 secluded wilderness campsites. Lake Nipigon is the biggest lake in Ontario other than the Great Lakes; with black sandy beaches, more than 1,000 islands, one Provincial Park, and God knows how many trout.

Lake Nipigon is also where the 1941 children's book "Paddle-to-the-Sea" was set. A wooden carving of an Indian canoe and paddler starts a journey in a stream running into Lake Nipigon, and ends up in France. Along the way it gets lost in a bag of laundry in Lake Michigan and goes over Niagara Falls. A nice story.

Northern Ontario is loaded with rivers. So it's loaded with river parks too: Turtle River-White Otter, Brightsand River, Kopia River, Pipestone River, Severn River, Fawn River, Otoskwin-Attawapiskat River, Albany River, Winisk River, Little Current River, Kesagami River, Little Abitibi River, Missinaibi River; and that's not all of them.

Paddle-to-the-Sea Waiting near Lake Nipigon for Snow to melt and Journey to Start.

Then there are great big huge parks where you have to figure out how to actually get to them: Wabakimi, Opasquia.

But it's not just rivers, lakes and islands in Northern Ontario parks. There's the Trans-Provincial Snowmobile Trail system centred at Nipigon, 38,400 kilometres (24,000 miles) of wilderness trails just for snowmobiles too. You need a map for it. In fact they don't just have road maps in Northern Ontario, they have maps of parks and campgrounds; maps of hunting and fishing camps; and maps of canoe, snowmobile, hiking and cross-country skiing trails. (In 1931 three men from North Cobalt skied 560 kilometres [350 miles] down Yonge Street to Toronto in 11 days. On one pair of 18-foot-long skis).

Then there's the parks that specialize in animals. Woodland Caribou Provincial Park has a herd of Woodland caribou in it. And you can probably guess what Polar Bear Provincial Park has in it.

Polar Bear Provincial Park is 480 kilometres (300 miles) north of Moosonee on the shores of Hudson Bay. It's the largest, most remote, least developed and least visited park in Ontario. Other than 400 polar bears, it's also home to Lesser Snow geese, Black bear, Red fox, Arctic fox, wolf, otter, skunk, hare, beaver, muskrat, moose, caribou, Beluga whale, walrus, seal and 23,800 square kilometres (9,300 square miles).

It's a park bigger than Wales, Massachusetts or New Hampshire. A park you fly into with a special park permit. A park renowned for its biting and sucking insects. A park with little firewood. A park of flat muskeg, ponds, shallow lakes and not much dry land. A park visited by less than 1,000 people a year. A park that's like going to another country. For not only do you have to want to go to Polar Bear Provincial Park and make the effort to get there, but you also have to be able to convince the Park Superintendent in Cochrane that you are able to look after yourself once you're in there in order to get your park permit. A park that you need a visa to visit.

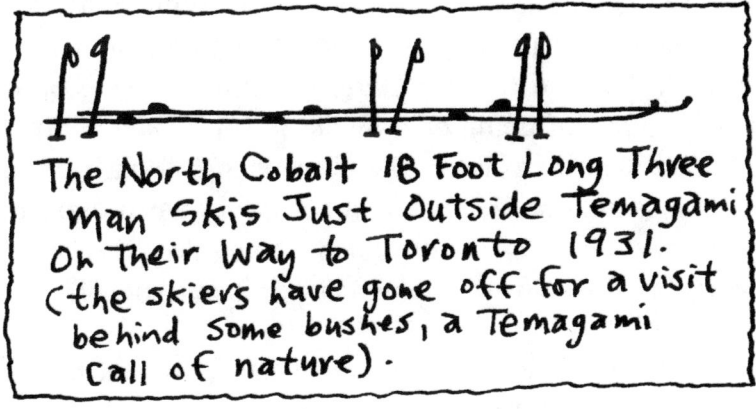

The North Cobalt 18 Foot Long Three man Skis Just Outside Temagami On Their Way to Toronto 1931. (the skiers have gone off for a visit behind some bushes, a Temagami call of nature).

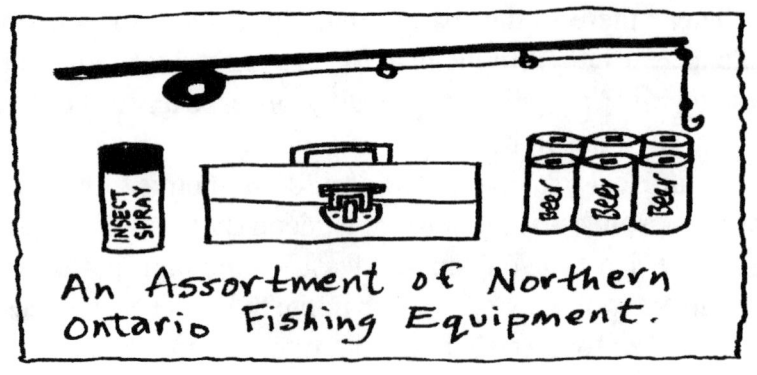

An Assortment of Northern Ontario Fishing Equipment.

CHAPTER EIGHTEEN
Lake Superior

Lake Superior is a lake with a good name. It's the biggest of the Great Lakes. The biggest of the Great. It's the biggest freshwater lake in the world. The biggest of the fresh. It's the Great Lake with the most shipwrecks in it. The biggest of the wrecks. It's the superior lake. Surprisingly however what Lake Superior isn't superior in is islands. There are no Thousand Islands in Lake Superior. There are two big islands and a few smaller ones. Lake Superior isn't known for islands. But the land north of Lake Superior makes up for it. With more lakes.

Somebody once sat down and counted all the lakes in Northern Ontario. When they got to two million they stopped. What's the sense of going on? What does it matter if you've actually got 2.4 million lakes or 3 million lakes? What's another hundred thousand lakes here or there? Anyway when somebody now asks the question: "how many lakes do they have in Northern Ontario anyway?" there's at least some sort of answer to give them.

Northern Ontario is floating in lakes. Ontario is the province with the highest percentage of its area composed of fresh water (16.6%), and most of it is up in Northern Ontario. In lakes. Why they even have a lake in Northern Ontario called "Lac des Mille Lacs" (Lake of a Thousand Lakes).

And most of these lakes in Northern Ontario are north of Lake Superior, especially north and west of Lake Superior. Northwestern Ontario actually looks to be more lake than land. Lakes with little bits of land in between. A land of lakes in the shadow of the greatest of the Great Lakes.

Some Great Lake too. Lake Superior is 560 kilometres (350 miles) long and 256 kilometres (160 miles) across. If you plopped all of New Brunswick into Lake Superior you'd still have enough water left over to make a swimming pool the size of one and a half Prince Edward Islands.

Not only is Lake Superior big, but it's also deep, 1,332 feet deep at its deepest. There's enough water in Lake Superior to irrigate all of North and South America to a depth of one foot. Lake Superior could grow a lot of rice.

In fact Lake Superior was so big and so deep that it was just too much lake for one country, so Canada and the U.S.A. decided to share it equally between them. The U.S.A. got two-thirds of the lake, the biggest island and the mainly flat, sandy beaches of the south shore; while Canada got one-third of the lake, the second biggest island, and the rugged, sheer rock cliffs and deep bays of the north shore. A fair sharing. The U.S.A. got the volume. Canada got the scenery.

When the Group of Seven had painted their way up and down the Algoma Central Railway line and were looking for more scenery to paint, they chose the scenery of Rossport, Jackfish, Coldwell and Pic Island on the far north shore of Lake Superior. The Group of Seven knew scenery when they saw it.

The land north of Superior is a land of water, deep water, clear water, cold water, fish, angry water, rocks, jagged rocks, smooth rocks, fish, round rocks, round boulders, round stones, round pebbles, fish, cliffs, mountains, rivers, fish, rapids, islands, snow, ice, fish, ice-fishing, storms, squalls, trees, forests, fish, wilderness, lakes, big lakes, little lakes, fish lakes, sunsets over lakes, lakes with names, lakes without names, lakes to fish in, parks, the odd human settlement, and of course fish.

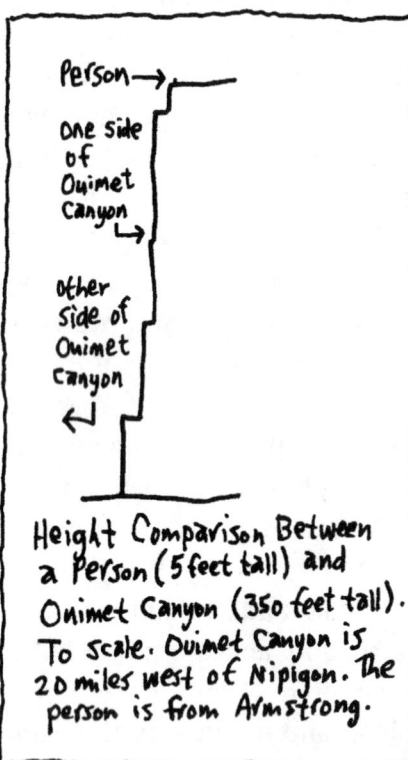

To say that they have fishing in Northern Ontario is an understatement. Just about everywhere you cast your hook in Northern Ontario there's a lake with a fish waiting for it at the other end. You can fish on your own or try the Northern Ontario speciality: the fly-in fishing camp. Here's just a sample of how some of the Northern Ontario fishing lodges describe their fishing: "Great fishing -- muskie, pike, pickerel, trout, bass, perch;" "Discover the excitement of catching bragging-class walleye or that trophy pike that has managed to elude you;" "Fully equipped boats and motors, fish seven lakes for seven species of fish;" "Huge lake trout, giant pike, succulent walleye, evasive bass and the world's best trophy brook trout;" "World class speckled trout."

Needless to say if you like fishing, Northern Ontario is one of the world Meccas of fishing, and many people come just to fish. Or to watch other people fish, which is equally relaxing.

Chapter Nineteen

A Fort and a Port and a Last Resort

Official Club Hat Shuniah Snowshoe Club, Port Arthur 1890. (tassel not optional)

Approach Thunder Bay from the east or west and it will seem like a pretty big place. It's the biggest city between Winnipeg and Sault Ste. Marie (1,366 kilometres, 854 miles, Winnipeg is 6.5 kilometres, four miles closer), yet it's only Canada's 25th largest city. It only seems bigger than it is because the other towns between Winnipeg and Sault Ste. Marie are smaller.

Thunder Bay is the biggest city in Northwestern Ontario. Sudbury is the biggest city in Northeastern Ontario. Yet if you put either of them in the outskirts of Toronto you'd hardly even notice them (you hardly even notice Markham). Yet up in Northern Ontario they're the biggest things around. Which is really what led to "The Battle of Northwestern Ontario."

Thunder Bay is actually the new name for two old towns with two old names: Fort William and Port Arthur, as listed alphabetically; or Port Arthur and Fort William, as listed north to south. At one time you had to be very careful about how you referred to these two towns. Show the slightest favouritism towards one, and the other was automatically against you.

They were neighbours, but they were rivals. They were roommates, but they were competitors. They were twin cities, but only because they were beside each other. Compared to them the twin cities of Kitchener-Waterloo were little angels. They fought with each other. They ignored each other. They didn't cooperate with each other. It all had to do with "The Battle of Northwestern Ontario." The battle to see who would become the

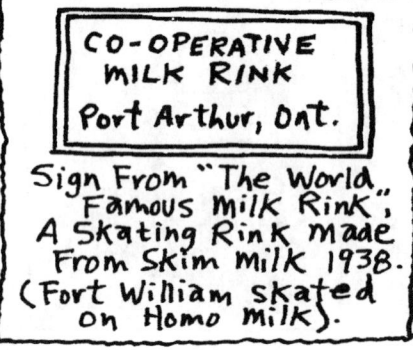

Sign From "The World Famous Milk Rink", A Skating Rink Made From Skim Milk 1938. (Fort William skated on Homo milk).

biggest fish in the Northeastern Ontario pond. And it was just between the two of them. The Fort versus The Port. There was no other challenger. Their only opponent was on the other side of William Street.

The Battle of Northwestern Ontario lasted for 165 years. And in the end the winner was neither of them. It was a new fish by the name of Thunder Bay.

In order to understand The Battle of Northwestern Ontario you need to know that the original Fort William fort was not where it is today. The original Fort William fort was built on the Kaministiquia River close to the lake (present day McTavish Street). But the reconstructed Fort William fort that you can visit today is 11 kilometres (seven miles) east of the lake (there wasn't enough room left on McTavish Street).

So this is why the original town site of Fort William was called West Fort William, because it was west of the original fort (West Fort William is today east of the reconstructed fort). Fort William as a town then grew west along the river, not north along the lake.

The original Port Arthur port was built five kilometres (three miles) north of the Kaministiquia River beside the lake (present day Red River Road). Port Arthur as a town then grew west from the lake, not south along it.

So the two towns grew away from each other, not towards each other. If they hadn't then perhaps they would have become one town sooner than they did. But they didn't. So we had The Battle of Northwestern Ontario. Probably the best scrap between two towns Canada has ever seen.

In the beginning though there was just Fort Caministogoyan on the Kaministiquia River. Everything was simple (except for the spelling of Caministogoyan and Kaministiquia).

The French built Fort Caministogoyan in 1679. Then they left and didn't come back again until 1717. Fort Caministogoyan was not in good shape (wood forts don't last forever). So they built a new fort and called it Fort Kaministiquia. This made things even simpler (there was no need to spell Caministogoyan any more).

A Port Arthur Winter Water Delivery Sleigh, 1909. (no deliveries south of South Water Street).

After the Seven Years War (1754-1760), the French abandoned Fort Kaministiquia (the French had lost the Seven Years War), and the British came to the west end of Lake Superior (the British had won the Seven Years War). But the British ignored Fort Kaministiquia and built a new fur trading post further south on the Pigeon River (Pigeon is much easier to spell and pronounce than Kaministiquia).

After the American Revolution (1775-1783), the Pigeon River became the Canada/U.S.A. border, so the British moved back north to Fort Kaministiquia (the British had lost the

American Revolution). Not willing to completely obliterate local history altogether, the British kept the name Kaministiquia for the river (but when they found out it could also be spelled "Kaministikwia" they took to calling it the "River Kam" for short); but changed the name of the fort to Fort William (1805), for which generations of Thunder Bay residents and tourists alike have been forever grateful.

An Old Log Similar To The Type Used To Build Old Fort William 1807 (horizontal variety)

Tourists to the Thunder Bay Tourism Office asking about visiting the 42 buildings on the 125 acres of the 1815 reconstruction of Old Fort William, are just as thankful that they don't have to ask about visiting Old Fort Kaministiquia as the tourism people are that they don't have to tell tourists how to pronounce it.

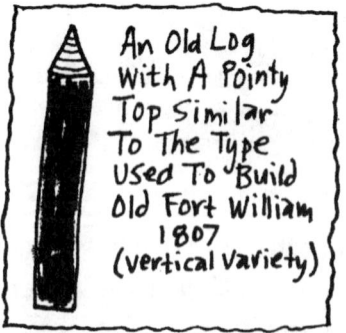
An Old Log With A Pointy Top Similar To The Type Used To Build Old Fort William 1807 (vertical variety)

It was just after 1805 however that things started to get complicated. Some people began using a spot on the shore five kilometres (three miles) north of Fort William as a landing place for shipping. They called this place "The Depot." They chose it because the water was deeper and stayed open longer and froze over later than the river. It was the beginning of The Battle of Northwestern Ontario. The Fort versus The Port. At this point though Fort William had the advantage because it was a fort that took six years to build and "presented an engaging exterior," while Port Arthur was called The Depot and was nothing more than a spot on a shore.

In 1857 an expedition sent to find the best route from Lake Superior to Winnipeg, chose as its starting point the higher location overlooking "Thunder Bay" (The Depot), rather than the lower, swampy land around the river (Fort William). This then was the first reference to the name "Thunder Bay" (in use since 1662).

When the Canadian army was on its way to the Red River Rebellion (1870), they too chose The Depot and renamed it "Prince Arthur's Landing." On their way back they built a fort here and called it "Fort Arthur." The fort was never used except as a source of logs to build houses with, and the name was never used either, probably because it had the word "Fort" in it.

In 1875 the Canadian Pacific Railway chose Fort William as its terminal. Some people from Prince Arthur's Landing were invited to the sod-turning ceremony. Some weren't. A group of those that weren't stole the official shovel and wheelbarrow, cut their own sod, and took everything back to The Landing. Fort William was not happy. The Landing was happy.

The Official Fort William Sod-Turning Shovel 1875. (it eventually ended up in New York with a former Port Arthur druggist).

The Landing then built their own railway to Fort William so it could connect with the CPR. Fort William was not happy. The Landing was happy. But the CPR would not let the railway connect. The Landing was not happy. Fort William was happy. But The Landing connected anyway. Fort William was not happy. The Landing was happy.

The two towns' newspapers fought too. The Landing called Fort William: "A swamp of sneaks. No place for a town. It has taken a century and a quarter to become a hamlet. Until it is decided whether the ground is to belong to aquatic things or to human beings, it might be well not to speak of a rival town."

Fort William called The Landing: "An ant hill. The people seem to do very little of anything but drink whisky. There are four lawyers and it is no uncommon sight to see the whole lot of them whooping around the streets at once" (there were actually five lawyers, but only one of them had never served a term in jail).

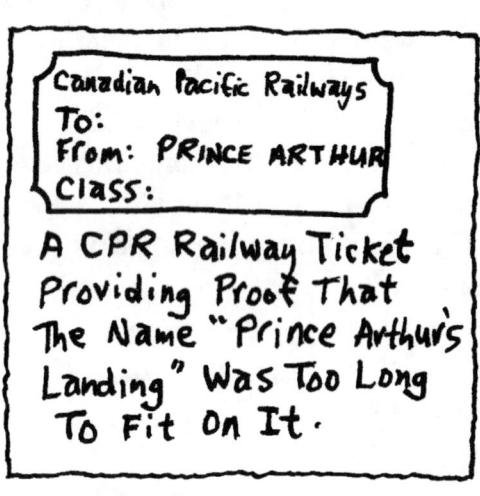

But Prince Arthur's Landing had not given up on getting the CPR. So when the railway hinted that it might be nice if their Lake Superior terminal were named "Port," and that the name Prince Arthur's Landing was too long to fit on a railway ticket, The Landing changed its name to Port Arthur (1882). But the CPR went to Fort William anyway.

So Port Arthur incorporated as a town (1884), beating The Fort to town status by eight years. It also had 38 liquor licenses to The Fort's nine. The railway came to The Port. But The Port seized a railway engine in lieu of unpaid taxes, and the railway moved to The Fort. The Port was not happy. The Fort was happy.

The Port proposes a streetcar line between the two towns. The Fort says they can bring their passengers to the town boundary and then they could "hoof it the balance of the way." The Port builds its streetcar line anyway. The Fort becomes a town: "The biggest port is William Fort, on this great inland sea;" but the province also gives The Port permission to built its streetcar line into The Fort. The Port lays tracks. The Fort pulls them up. But part of the Port (West Fort) wants the streetcars. So The Port lays tracks all the way to the River Kam. Part of The Fort was not happy. The Port was happy.

But the contest is now getting dangerous. The two towns do everything separately. The Fort's water comes from the river and Loch Lomond Lake. The Port's water comes from wells and Lake Superior. There is a diptheria outbreak in The Port. The Fort requires streetcar passengers from The Port to have a health card. A Port newspaper editor punches a Fort doctor. The editor is fined for assault. The doctor is fined for abusive language.

There is a smallpox outbreak on a train heading to The Port and The Fort. Both towns refuse permission for the train to stop. The train goes back and forth between The Port and The Fort before a doctor takes charge.

Fire breaks out in The Fort, but the fire hose only stretches 1,000 feet from the river and their power company burns down. The Fort takes power from The Port's streetcar line. When a movie is showing in a theatre in The Fort and a streetcar goes by, the movie stops. A joint power project fails when The Port's mayor "refused or neglected to sign the contract." (The Port has its own power).

By 1900 the combined population of The Fort and The Port is only 6,000. The Port was "The Silver Gateway." The Fort was "The Gold Gateway." But cows grazed on the streets and pigs walked on the sidewalks.

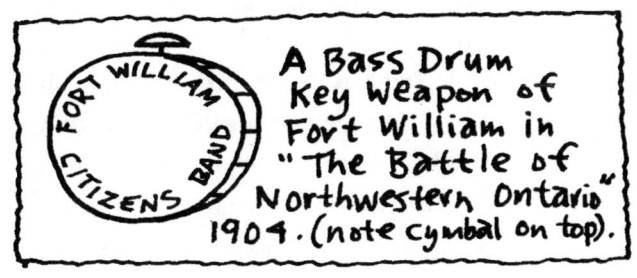

A Bass Drum Key Weapon of Fort William in "The Battle of Northwestern Ontario" 1904. (note cymbal on top).

In 1906 both towns apply to become cities. The province is dragged into the squabble. The Premier threatens to resign rather than listen to any more Fort/Port demands. They become separate cities (1907). It is now feuding cities not feuding towns. There are amalgamation votes in 1920 and 1958. The Port votes yes, The Fort votes no, both times.

The federal government is dragged into the squabble. The Port wants breakwaters. The Fort wants dredging. Ottawa loses patience. Tired of dealing with two harbours controlled by two cities whose sole purpose is to outdo each other, they pass federal legislation creating a new single harbour authority whose name hasn't got the words "Fort," "Port," "William" or "Arthur" in it. It's called "The Lakehead Harbour Commission." It's the world's largest freshwater port (before it was just half the world's largest freshwater port). The Fort and The Port are not happy.

In 1968 Toronto loses patience too. The two cities *will* amalgamate and their new name *will not* have the words "Fort," "Port," "William" or "Arthur" in it either. Their new name will be "The City of The Lakehead," like it or lump it. They pass the bill in 1969. The Battle of Northwestern Ontario is over. Finished. Or is it?

The Fort and The Port are not happy. They agree on something for the very first time. Two things actually. They want to vote on their new name, and they do not want to be called Kaministiquia or The Depot. The province permits them to vote on a new name. The three choices are: "Lakehead," "The Lakehead" or "Thunder Bay." Thunder Bay wins but there are more votes for the Lakehead with or without the "The." There is a squabble over vote-rigging. The ballots are destroyed. They do not want to know who voted for what. It doesn't matter any more. The Battle of Northwestern Ontario is almost over (they call the university "Lakehead" to make up for it).

The province accepts their new name and on 1 January 1970 the new city of Thunder Bay is created. The Battle of Northwestern Ontario is well and truly over. They were one city now. One happy city. A city with mountains behind and a Sleeping Giant in front. A city with a nice new name. Of course they could have had it 165 years ago if they'd wanted.

After amalgamation things were less exciting at the west end of Lake Superior. Trains still ran. Grain elevators still elevated. Pulp and paper mills still pulped and milled. There was a Thunder Bay North and a Thunder Bay South. The university was in the north. The city hall was in the south. But nobody cared any more. Don't believe it.

Modern Day Weapons Used In "The Battle of Thunder Bay" 1970 –

Today in Thunder Bay people beat each other over the head with hockey sticks, curling brooms, skiis and baseball bats. They're crazy about sports in Thunder Bay. It's the only way they've got left to see who's the biggest fish in the Thunder Bay pond.

So when you're in Thunder Bay try to stay out of the way of flying sports equipment. And never say those two old names. It's the only way to stay neutral. For staying neutral in Thunder Bay is still the most important thing to do.

The Sleeping Giant is the name given to the rock formation on the Sibley Peninsula, 24 kilometres (15 miles) across the bay from the city. But it's not the only rock formation near Thunder Bay.

Agate is a semi-precious stone of swirling circles in different colours. You can hunt for your own agate at the Thunder Bay Agate Mine, or at the agate gift shop.

Amethyst is a semi-precious stone of purple crystals. The biggest amethyst mine in North America is at Elbow Lake, 56 kilometres (35 miles) east of Thunder Bay. You can hunt for your own amethysts at the mine or at the Amethyst Factory Gift Shop in Thunder Bay.

Amethyst is the official mineral of Ontario. Long before that it was used by Egyptians in amulets; adopted as the birthstone for February; and declared the official gem for Wednesday, Pisces and Jupiter.

Oddly enough they've found that amethyst hunting in Thunder Bay is especially popular with Egyptians born on a Wednesday in February under the sign of Pisces, and with all tourists from Jupiter.

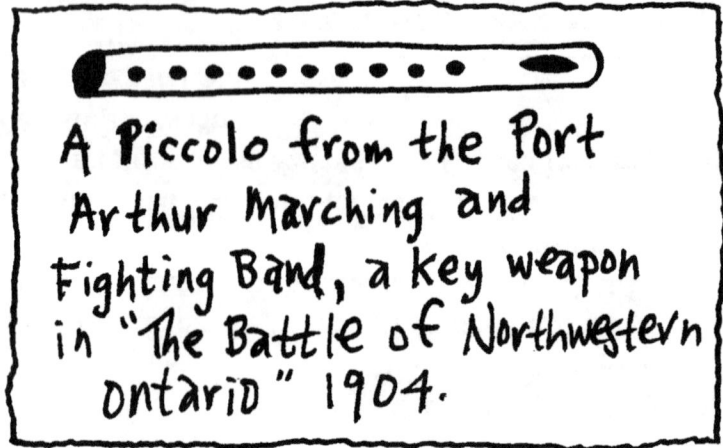

A Piccolo from the Port Arthur Marching and Fighting Band, a key weapon in "The Battle of Northwestern Ontario" 1904.

Chapter Twenty

The Land on the Other Side of the Time Zone

Just 64 kilometres (40 miles) west of Thunder Bay something happens that doesn't happen in any other province in Canada. You enter another time zone. You go from Eastern Time to Central Time. Ontario time to Manitoba time. Thunder Bay time to Winnipeg time. Yet you're still in the same province.

Thunder Bay is in the same time zone as Toronto, Ottawa and Moonbeam, Ontario. But Atikokan, Fort Frances, Rainy River, Ignace, Dryden, Sioux Lookout, Pickle Lake, Red Lake and Kenora are all in the same time zone as Winnipeg, Brandon and Snowflake, Manitoba.

A different world. The land still looks the same as Northern Ontario, but the further west you go the stronger becomes the pull of the time zone. The pull of Manitoba. The pull of Winnipeg.

A Canoe Carrying Vital Summer Supplies in Quetico Provincial Park Just Outside Atikokan (the canoeist has gone off for a visit behind some bushes, a Quetico call of nature).

Atikokan was just a little place out in the bush in the 1940s when they found iron ore nearby. There's a mining museum in Atikokan, but today it's better known as "The Canoeing Capital of Canada." The town is adjacent to Quetico Provincial Park. A canoeists' park. A park with some of the best wilderness canoeing in the world. A park where you can canoe to Minnesota.

Fort Frances was the furthest west the voyageur fur traders could paddle from Montreal and still make it back east again before the route froze up. Today you can visit the reconstructed Fort Saint Pierre at Fort Frances, the point of no return for the voyageurs.

Rainy River is equidistant between Winnipeg and Thunder Bay. But Winnipeg is the 8th largest city in Canada and Thunder Bay is 25th. And Minnesota is right over there. Rainy River is also the end of Yonge Street. Yonge Street started out in

Toronto and ended up 1,885.28 kilometres (1,178.3 miles) later in Rainy River. It also ended up in the Guiness Book of Records as "the longest street in the world."

Ignace was named after Ignace Mentour, a Caughnawaga Indian from Montreal who guided canoe expeditions for Sir Sandford Fleming (Canadian Pacific Railways and inventor of the time zones), and Sir George Simpson (Hudson's Bay Company). Ignace Mentour had a way of picking distinguished people. Distinguished people had a way of picking Ignace Mentour.

At first Ignace was just a little dot on the CPR line between Falcon and Butler. Today Ignace is the biggest dot on the Trans-Canada Highway between Thunder Bay and Dryden (Falcon and Butler meanwhile have disappeared off the map).

In 1909 they considered changing the name of Ignace to Elmsdale. This would have been a great shame since Elmsdale sounds like it should be a suburb of Oakville; whereas Ignace sounds like it should be a town on the Canadian Shield with hunting and fishing and parks nearby, which is as things turned out, just exactly what it is.

Dryden is equidistant between Winnipeg and Thunder Bay. But the call of the Manitoba bison is strong. The call of the Dryden moose is strong too. Dryden has an 18-foot-tall moose called Maximillian which stands guard over the town (lots of Northern Ontario towns have adopted giant animals).

In 1910 a survey was undertaken which reached the conclusion that there were only three areas suitable for agriculture in the whole of Northwestern Ontario: Rainy River, Kenora and Dryden. Thankfully somebody also noticed that there were trees growing around Dryden, with the result that Dryden became a pulp and paper, lumbering and printing town as well as a home for an oversized moose.

Sioux Lookout is not at the end of a one-way road. It is

possible to leave Sioux Lookout by a road other than the one you came in on, but it doesn't get you very far unless you want to get onto the one-way road to Pickle Lake.

Sioux Lookout is also 170 kilometres (106 miles) away from Sioux Narrows. The one thing Sioux Lookout and Sioux Narrows have in common is Sioux. At Sioux Lookout the Ojibway Indians kept a lookout for the Sioux Indians, and defeated a raiding party of them here. At Sioux Narrows the Ojibway again defeated the Sioux. The Sioux were Plains Indians from the U.S.A. who came to Canada and eventually settled in Southern Manitoba where they got a more hospitable reception than they got in Northern Ontario, even if they did have two towns named after them.

Pickle Lake is 290 kilometres (181 miles) north of the Trans-Canada Highway at the end of a one-way road. Pickle Lake is as far north as you can go in Northern Ontario on a good road. Yet Pickle Lake is still south of Saskatoon, Saskatchewan.

The people of Northwestern Ontario are pulled by the time zone west towards Manitoba more than they are pulled east towards the rest of Ontario. Toronto is some place down there. But Winnipeg is just down the road. Thunder Bay and Northwestern Ontario hardly seem like Ontario at all, except in one overwhelming respect. Geography. They share the same rocks, trees and lakes geography as the rest of Northern Ontario. Once you cross into Manitoba, however, the rocks, trees and lakes geography is soon left behind and replaced by the geography of the Prairies, another quite different geography altogether. It's actually quite a startling transformation. In terms of geography the Ontario/Manitoba boundary almost fits perfectly.

Chapter Twenty-One

Red Lake

Red Lake is 168 kilometres (105 miles) north of the Trans-Canada Highway at the end of a one-way road. At one time there was no road. But that didn't matter because nobody really wanted to go to Red Lake anyway.

Three Brown Pelicans on a Rock in Lac Seul (contemplating flying to Red Lake).

Fur traders went there from 1786-1806, 1816-1822, and then went back again in 1918 and stayed because Red Lake suddenly became a very exciting place to be in 1925, and the Hudson's Bay Company did a lot of business there selling things to prospectors, not fur traders.

In 1897 they found gold at Red Lake. Eight claims were staked, including some by Bill Tyrell, but nothing else happened. In 1922 they found silver at Red Lake. One hundred claims were staked, including some by Gus McManus, a little bit happened, but then all the claims lapsed and nothing else happened.

In 1924 the Ontario Department of Mines published a survey report on Red Lake. The report sat in their Toronto office. Lorne Howey from Haileybury was in Toronto in 1925, met a prospector who had been to Red Lake, and got a copy of this report.

When he got back to Haileybury he persuaded three others, including his brother Ray, to go to Red Lake. So in May 1925 the four of them loaded two canoes and their gear on the train and headed west. They got off at Hudson (west of Sioux Lookout), and paddled and portaged 288 kilometres (180 miles) in 5-6 days northwest to Red Lake. When they got there they found four other prospectors from Haileybury already there!

A lot of Canadian prospectors would go anywhere in the country if they got a sniff that something was up. Some of them would go anywhere in the world. Prospecting is an addiction. Like gambling. You gamble your money, stamina and smarts against Mother Nature. Mother Nature's hidden gold in the ground. Can you find it?

Northern Ontario is as big as Nigeria or Venezuela. But to the mining prospectors of Northern Ontario it's just their own personal prospecting playground to prospect in. Roads or no roads. Railway or no railway. Here were eight prospectors from the same small town, 1,120 kilometres (700 miles) away from home, on the same lake at the same time for the same reason. A lake out of the thousands of lakes that nobody had bothered much about before. Yet here they were.

After a month the first group left, but the Howey group stayed on. After almost two months of scratching around they found gold on the shores of what would be called Howey Bay. They staked 22 claims and returned to Haileybury in early September. When they got home they found that more prospectors from Haileybury and the District of Temiskaming had already left for Red Lake! They had to move fast. Not only fast, they had to move far.

All claims staked at Red Lake in the summer of 1925 had to be recorded at the Mining Recorder's Office in Kenora (269 kilometres, 168 miles south of Red Lake, no road), and have the required mining work started before winter set in. Otherwise the claims would expire. So Howey formed the Howey Gold Mine Syndicate and then did something that no other mining company in Canada had ever done before. They hired five flying boats from Sioux Lookout to fly men, equipment and supplies into Red Lake before winter. It was the first time aircraft had ever been used in mining. And it worked.

All the claims staked at Red Lake and recorded in Kenora in 1925 were made by Northern Ontario prospectors from Cobalt, Coniston (Sudbury) Fort William, Haileybury, Hudson, Sault Ste. Marie and South Porcupine; including Gus McManus who re-staked his old claims from 1922.

A small group celebrated the Christmas of 1925 together at Red Lake. But by the end of 1926 some 5,000 prospectors had come and gone, 6,000 claims had been staked, and the Red Lake Gold Rush was over. Only a small group celebrated the Christmas of 1926 together at Red Lake. Much the same group that had been there a year ago.

A lot of people know about the Yukon Gold Rush and the gold towns of Timmins and Kirkland Lake; but not a lot of people know about the Red Lake Gold Rush of 1926. It was all over in a flash. A last great hurrah. Red Lake was the last of the gold rushes. The last time hordes of ordinary, completely inexperienced people dropped everything and rushed off to the wilderness to seek their fortune (now they just buy a lottery ticket).

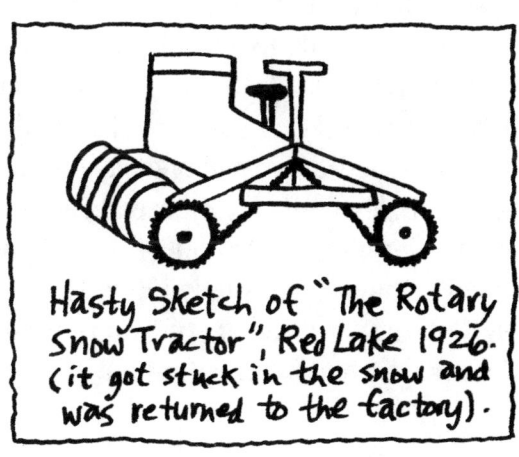

Hasty Sketch of "The Rotary Snow Tractor", Red Lake 1926. (it got stuck in the snow and was returned to the factory).

Prospecting is a technologically sophisticated business now. As the Kidd Creek Mine in Timmins showed. There's still a need to hike through the bush, of course, but now more prospecting is done from the air and the office, than it is with a hammer and a tent by a lake. There will be no more Cobalts. No more Porcupines. No more Kirkland Lakes. No more Red Lakes.

Red Lake is not as well known as the other gold towns because there were no instant fortunes here. No easy gold lying on the surface. No nuggets in pans. No lifting moss. No domes of gold. After one year and all the claims only the Howey Mine was actually doing any mining work. The Howey Mine took four years to come into production, and ten years later it was still the only mine at Red lake producing gold. The Howey mine closed in 1951, but by that time other mines were going. By 1970 Red Lake had far surpassed the Klondike and by 1974 had taken over from Timmins as the gold capital of Ontario. At one time there were 18 gold mines at Red Lake. Today there are still two. But Red Lake's exciting year was 1926. And what a year it was!

In the winter of 1926 the most popular way into Red Lake was by dog-sled (gravel road 1947, paved road 1960). It was estimated that between 5,000-8,000 dogs rushed off to mush in the Red Lake Gold Rush. Dogs who had never thought about being a sled-dog before suddenly found themselves on the CNR heading for Hudson to be a sled-dog. Breeds that had never been known for pulling sleds before, suddenly found that they were highly sought after as sled-dogs. On one day 53 dog teams were counted on the Red Lake Trail. Kennels emptied. The stray dog problem between Winnipeg and Thunder Bay disappeared (along with any other dogs that weren't nailed down).

Gordon Shearn was hired at Hudson to drive a dog team based on the fact that he had once, sometime, driven a dog team.

A Long Winter Overcoat Guarantee of a Good Job in Red Lake in 1926. (With a hood a really good job).

Shearn hired an assistant based on the fact that he was strong and had a long winter overcoat that he would share.

David Wilson left New Jersey, U.S.A. on the train for Hudson, and then walked to Red Lake in a suit and tie, overcoat, street shoes and galoshes. When he found out Red Lake was all staked out, he walked to Woman Lake and staked there. He felt the need to stake. Altogether he walked 456 kilometres (285 miles) in the same clothes he had walked out of the office in. He later stayed on in the area (it was agreeable for walking).

One Galosh Similar To The Pair of Galoshes That Walked To Red Lake in 1926. (the old buckle type)

Bill Tyrell's son re-staked the same claims his father had staked in 1897. Red Lake was a magnet for Klondike veterans. They came from Canada, U.S.A., Mexico, South Africa,

Australia and New Zealand to walk to Red Lake (it was a lot easier than the walk to Dawson City).

The Red Lake Transportation Company was formed. It consisted of 96 horses and 65 men. For every two loads of freight it carried, it had to carry 1½ loads of horse feed.

The transportation methods fit the season. In summer: boats, flying boats, canoes, horses and wagons, and the "marine railway" (tugs pulling barges which were floated onto railway flat cars and pulled across portages on railway tracks). In winter: dog teams, horses and sleighs, men pulling toboggans, caterpillar tractors pulling sleighs (they tried "snow motors" and "motor sleighs" but none of them worked), and little planes with skiis and open cockpits.

Little planes that felt the cold. So when the temperature was -29°C (-20°F) they did all they could to keep the little planes warm: turned them so the sun shone on their engine; put boiling water in their radiator, heated their spark plugs, warmed their anti-freeze and oil. Eventually they came up with the idea of building a portable hangar over the nose of the plane with a stove inside. It was the first engine block heater.

But pilots and passengers felt the cold too. So they had to leave Red Lake before the sun went down otherwise they might get caught in frozen slush or a night snowstorm.

A second air service flew a plane from New Jersey, U.S.A. to Red Lake via: Buffalo; Toronto; Sudbury (change wheels for skiis); Pogamasing Lake (forced landing, spent night at lumber camp); Chapleau (or close to it); Amyot; Lake Nipigon; Sioux Lookout (dinner with mayor and local dignitaries); Hudson; Red Lake. Total trip 21 days.

A little tent town formed at Red Lake. The Province opened a Mining Recorder's Office (tent), and an Ontario Provincial Police Office (tent), even though there was hardly any crime and more security was actually needed for cases of beer shipped into Red Lake than bricks of gold shipped out.

The Post Office started out in a tent and moved to a log cabin with extensions built for a general store and restaurant and another one for poker games. The first "street" in Red Lake was the trail between the Post Office tent and the Red Cross Hospital tent (now Howey Street).

> **To:** Ontario Land Surveys Branch, Toronto.
> **FROM:** Mining Recorder's Office (tent), Red Lake.
> **ATTENTION:** Miss Winnifred Kirkland.
>
> Please send more forms A.S.A.P. and pencils if you can spare them!

Copy of First Air Mail Letter Sent From Red Lake 1926.

The new Mining Recorder's Office (tent) ran out of claim forms on the first day, so the first air mail letter sent from Red Lake was a request to Toronto for more forms. The letter flew to Hudson and was then trained to Toronto arriving in under four days (Canada Post has never since duplicated this feat).

With no forms left the Mining Recorder's Office (tent) gave people the one remaining blank form and a sheet of paper and asked them to copy out the form and return it for somebody else to copy from. In one day they processed 163 claims. Pencils were in short supply. Most prospectors only had a thick carpenter's pencil, not a writing pencil. Some people couldn't write, and one company had 60 claims to record and only one pencil.

George Punker was working on a Great Lakes freighter when he caught gold fever, took the train to Hudson, and pulled a toboggan to Red Lake. One of the things he took along was a typewriter. When he found out the Mining Recorder's Office (tent) had run out of forms, he set up his typewriter in a tent and typed out forms for $1 each.

In the year 1926 Red Lake captured the attention of the world's press. They followed the plane flights (aviation was still something new), the Gold Rush, and the drama (plane crash, dog bites, frostbite). There were big ideas about roads and railways to Red Lake, but nothing happened. Prospectors sat around in the spring waiting for the snow to melt so they could see what was underneath their claim. And when the snow returned everybody except the little group celebrating Christmas 1926 was gone.

But Red Lake's still there. At the end of a long, paved, one-way road. And there's still gold at Red Lake, so Red Lake just carries on quietly mining it. On a lake where some Indians once shot a giant creature which then fell into the lake and coloured the water red with its blood.

CUT YOUR OWN WOOD AND IT WILL WARM YOU TWICE.

Sign Over The Fireplace At The Hudson's Bay Company Post, Red Lake 1935.
(digging for gold only warms you once)

Chapter Twenty-Two

Kenora

Kenora is 56 kilometres (35 miles) from Manitoba and 203 kilometres (127 miles) from Winnipeg (practically a suburb). Kenora is also on The Lake of the Woods.

Husky the Musky Largest Fish Ever Caught in The Lake of the Woods. Stuffed and mounted in Kenora.

The Lake of the Woods is a very unusual lake. It's a lake where it's difficult to tell where the lake stops and starts. It's a lake of 14,632 islands (at last count), and 96,000 kilometres (60,000 miles) of shoreline. A lake of narrow channels and peninsulas that look like islands. A lake that's ¾ the size of Prince Edward Island, but which appears in some places to be more land than lake. It's a lake that's shared equally between Canada and the U.S.A. Canada has 72% of the lake and the U.S.A. has 28%. It's a lake quite unlike any other lake. And it's all because of Wendigo.

Wendigo was an Indian god. A lesser god. A god who really didn't have an important job to do. So one day just for fun he decided to make a garden in a lake. He filled the lake with islands. He planted trees, shrubs and plants. He scattered minerals around. He painted rocks. He made four lakes join into one. He made the lake into a maze. He made the waters a different colour.

After he was finished he was so pleased with what he had created that he turned himself into a rock in the middle of the lake so he could gaze forever at it and be amused by how humans coped with it.

Wendigo got a lot of amusement out of The Lake of the Woods. People got lost in its channels and amongst its islands. They chased after its minerals. They gave different names to the lake because they thought they were different lakes (Lake of the Sand Hills, Lake of the Islands, Whitefish Lake). And because Kenora was a town on The Lake of the Woods it got caught up in the magic of Wendigo too.

The Hudson's Bay Company originally named the town "Rat Portage." This was quite a colourful and unique name based on the fact that muskrats migrated across land here to get between the lake and the Winnipeg River. (Muskrats were fooled by The Lake of the Woods too. They could have done the trip by water if they'd been able to find the right channel, but The Lake of the Woods was a confusing lake, even for muskrats).

The Hudson's Bay Company sent surveyors to survey the town too (1878). A town on The Lake of the Woods. A town on a complicated lake. A town beside a lake with an irregular shoreline, islands, bays, rivers, creeks, channels and little lakes. A town beside a lake on

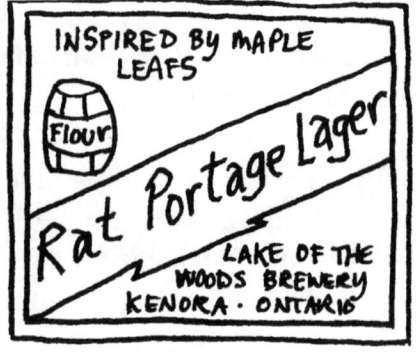

land that was hilly, rocky and uneven. And the surveyors only knew how to survey straight lines. So, despite the fact that there was hardly any straight land to survey straight lines on, they surveyed Kenora as a town of straight lines.

As a result Water Street in Kenora hardly gets going (one short block) before it has to stop (because of water). Main Street runs parallel with Water Street but at one time didn't go very far either (several uneven blocks) before it too had to stop (because of railway tracks). When they eventually removed these tracks Main Street continued in a straight line as Main Street S. before it had to bend left around the river, make a 90° turn to the right, cross more railway tracks, and continue on the other side as Main Street N. (Lots of streets in Kenora have North and South parts, whether they run north-south and are called Streets or Avenues; or east-west and are called Streets or Avenues).

Matheson Street S. runs parallel with Water Street and Main Street S. goes several uneven blocks, crosses over the railway tracks, and then runs straight into 1st St. N., which is itself only a few (uneven) blocks long and dead-ended at both ends. Matheson St. S. then continues as Matheson St. N.

The beer labels shown are a selection of Kenora beer labels that never went into production.

(from a private collection)

after doing a little S-bend because Matheson St. S. and Matheson St. N. do not line up with one another. (Lots of streets in Kenora have the same name but do not line up with one another, and in some cases don't have anything to do with each other at all).

1st St. S. is south of the railway tracks (but not the first street south of the tracks), and is now in three parts none of which line up with each other (two short parts and one longer part). They could have been named 1st St. S. East, and 1st St. S. West, and 1st St. S. Middle; but that would have been too complicated, even for Kenora. 1st St. S. is also not the original 1st St. S., that's now 3rd St. S. 1st St. S. is not the first street south of the railway tracks because McClellan Avenue is (another shortish street of two uneven blocks), but 1st St. N. is definitely the first street north of the tracks.

River Street is in two parts, neither of which has anything remotely to do with the other. One part runs along the river in the north end of town (before joining into 9th St. N.); while the other part runs along a creek in the south side of town, not even close to the river, and completely divorced from the other part of River Street altogether. Wendigo certainly got a lot of amusement out of watching them plan the streets of Kenora. But he wasn't finished yet.

Things were going along nicely in Rat Portage until 1905 when the Maple Leaf Flour Company told the town that it would never build a flour mill in a town where the word "rat" had to appear on its flour bags. So Rat Portage changed its name to Kenora (jobs before rats).

Kenora is a made-up name. A name made up by using the first two letters of "Keewatin" (a nearby town), the first two letters of "Norman" (another nearby town), and the first two letters of the name the Maple Leaf Flour Company didn't like (the town did have its principles).

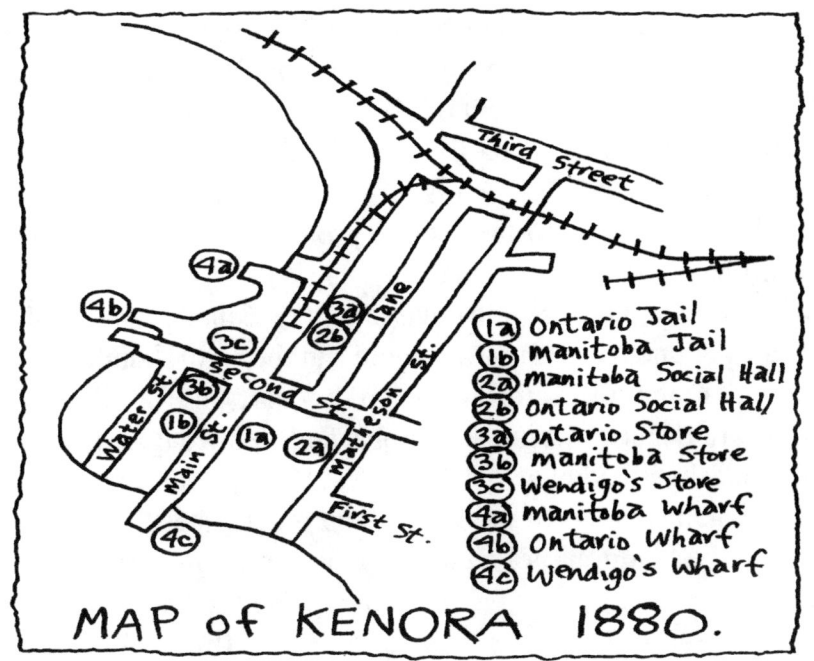

After Kenora got its streets and its name settled, they couldn't decide who ran the town, the railway company or the government. Both had their own police force, jails and fines.

A railway constable seized illegal liquor, drank it himself, and was arrested by the government magistrate and fined. The railway constable then arrested the government magistrate for the same offence and put him in the railway jail. A new government magistrate was appointed who then fined the old government magistrate. Wendigo at work.

After Kenora got its streets, name and local government sorted out, they couldn't decide which province it should be in: Manitoba or Ontario. So it spent some time in both. Kenora was incorporated in Manitoba in 1882 and in Ontario in 1892. But the problem started in 1870.

Kenora was minding its own business as the biggest town between Fort Garry (Winnipeg) and Fort William (Thunder Bay), when the government of Canada came along and created the province of Manitoba. But they didn't make it big enough. It was only 1/24th the size it is now, and everybody laughed at it and called it "the postage stamp province" . . . so of course Manitoba wanted to get bigger.

So when in 1881 the government of Canada said that the western boundary of Ontario should run through Thunder Bay, Manitoba happily agreed, set up a court in Rat Portage, incorporated the town into Manitoba, and claimed it for its own. But Ontario already had a court in Rat Portage. So once again Kenora had two sets of policemen and magistrates.

The Manitoba police arrested the Ontario magistrates and police, and the Ontario police arrested the Manitoba magistrates and police. When the two provinces held elections the people of Kenora voted in both. When a man was arrested by Manitoba for operating a business without a licence (he had an Ontario licence), his friends broke into the Manitoba jail, set him free, and put the Manitoba officials in the Ontario jail.

A Little Sailing Boat Lost on The Lake of the Woods (the sailor has gone off to get directions).

It was all fun and games in Kenora. And it was all Wendigo's fault. Canada tried to solve the problem but couldn't, so finally in 1884 the Privy Council of England set the Manitoba/Ontario boundary along the 95° W longitude line (the present boundary), and put an end to it once and for all.

But Wendigo's fun wasn't over yet. Having created a provincial boundary dispute with The Lake of the Woods, he now created an international border dispute too.

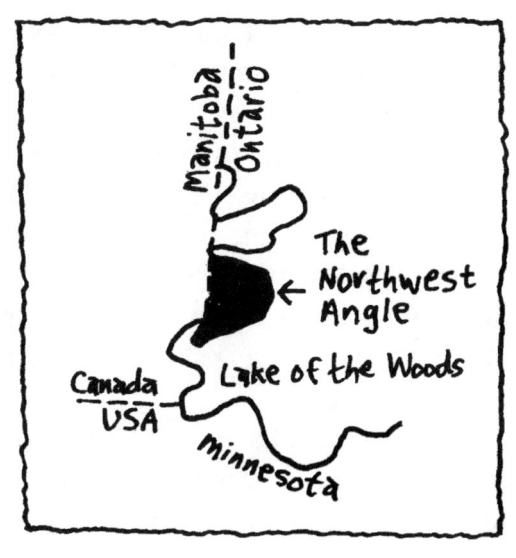

The Northwest Angle is a little bit of the state of Minnesota, U.S.A. which sticks out into The Lake of the Woods, is attached to Manitoba, but is on the Ontario side of the provincial boundary. The only way in or out of the Northwest Angle of Minnesota is through Canada. If it sounds confusing, it is.

After the American Revolution (1783) it was decided that the Canada/U.S.A. border should "follow the Rainy River to The Lake of the Woods, thence through said lake to the most northwestern part thereof, and from thence on due west course to the river Mississippi." (Wendigo probably had a hand in writing this).

But there were two problems with this description: the Mississippi River is south of The Lake of the Woods, not west; and where exactly on the lake was its "northwestern part?"

It wasn't until 1872 (90 years later), that a point on the lake was agreed upon. But when the rest of the Canada/U.S.A. border was established along the 49° latitude line (the line that now forms the Canada/U.S.A. border from Manitoba to British Columbia), it left a small peninsula of land north of this line still in the U.S.A. Quite a mess. And all Wendigo's fault.

The Northwest Angle is just one of several boo-boos that have been made along the Canada/U.S.A. border. Two others are the state of Maine, which sticks up too far north into Canada; and the Alaska panhandle, which sticks down too far south. (Wendigo however was not to blame for these.)

Today Wendigo is still having fun with Kenora and The Lake of the Woods. Every year they hold The Lake of the Woods Regatta, a sailing race around the lake starting at Kenora. And every year sailors and boaters get lost in the maze which is this lake.

You may think that it's the wind whistling through the trees, or the waves slapping upon the shore. But it's Wendigo chuckling. The Lake of the Woods is a very unusual lake indeed.

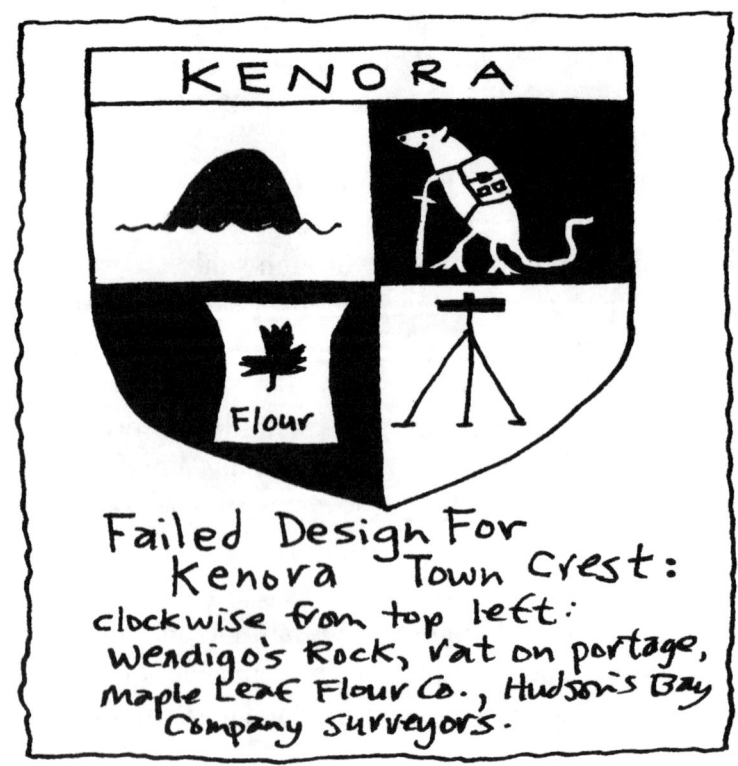

Failed Design For Kenora Town Crest: clockwise from top left: Wendigo's Rock, rat on portage, Maple Leaf Flour Co., Hudson's Bay Company surveyors.

About the Author

Geoffrey Corfield does not live in Northern Ontario. That's just the way things turned out. But he does have a friend in Elliot Lake. And he does know people who used to live in Kapuskasing, Kenora, North Bay, Sault Ste. Marie, Sudbury and Timmins. And while at university he went on a field trip to the District of Temiskaming and played soccer at Laurentian University. And when he lived out west he once did the trip the long way, over the top through Northern Ontario, just to see what it was like. And he can quite honestly say that having done this book, Northern Ontario's got more colour and character in its little finger than a lot of other places have got in their whole suburbs.

Geoffrey Corfield writes **INKBLOT**, a weekly Canadian humour column: 500 words, 1 limerick, 1 drawing, once a week since 1993; and produces **INKBLOT** postcards. This is the second in a series of **INKBLOT** travel books. The first one was on the Niagara Peninsula. He doesn't live there either.

Need a great gift for a friend?

Or want a fun read for yourself?

Order a copy of MORE *Great Canadian Fishing Stories That Didn't Get Away*, a collection of two dozen true and not-so-true fishing stories by eight of Canada's most popular outdoor writers.

▶ Only $16.95*
at all bookstores

▶ Only $16.95*
Send e-mail requests to:

despub@niagara.com
(Shipping included!)

▶ Only $16.95* from DESPUB, 2340B Clifton Street, Allanburg ON L0S 1A0 **(Shipping included!)**
   * **Plus, of course, GST**

Geoffrey Corfield has also written: The Niagara Peninsula: *There's More To Niagara Than Just Going Over The Falls In A Barrel.*

It's the "New and Improved" Second edition and its 112 pages are lavishly illustrated with the author's drawings.

It's a travel book/history lesson crammed with quirky humour and little-known historical trivia that helps explain why the Americans couldn't capture Canada!

- Only $14.95* at all bookstores

- Only $14.95* Send e-mail requests to: despub@niagara.com (Shipping included!)

- Only $14.95* from **DESPUB**, 2340B Clifton Street, Allanburg ON L0S 1A0 (Shipping included!)

* Plus, of course, GST

The Third Edition of *Ontario Place Names* is now available from DESPUB ! ! !

It contains the historical, offbeat or humorous origins of 1,180 communities, 30% more places than earlier editions, and all the unusual names, regardless of population.

This handy reference not only explains the origins of the communities' names, but gives current populations and locations, all major historical events, bizarre and humourous incidents and tells about famous people through history from explorers to sports stars, from inventors to wily entrepreneurs.

- Only $19.95* at all bookstores

- Only $19.95* Send e-mail requests to: despub@niagara.com **(Shipping included!)**

- Only $19.95* from **DESPUB**, 2340B Clifton Street, Allanburg ON L0S 1A0 **(Shipping included!)**
  * **Plus, of course, GST**

MEMBER OF THE SCABRINI MEDIA
Quebec, Canada
2002